If you are running your own business then you probably do not have time for the general, theoretical and often impenetrable subject areas covered by many business and management books. What works for the major corporation may not work for you. What you do need is to-the-point guidance on how to implement sound business skills in a growing enterprise.

The NatWest Business Handbooks deliver this practical advice in an easy-to-follow format.

Written by authors with many years' experience and who are still actively involved in the day-to-day running of successful businesses, these handbooks provide all the guidance you need to tackle the everyday issues that you and your business face. They will enable you to adopt a step-by-step approach to isolating and resolving problems and help you meet the entrepreneurial and organisational challenges of a growing business.

♻ NatWest

BUSINESS HANDBOOKS

SMALL BUSINESS SURVIVAL

Strategies for delivering growth and staying profitable

Second Edition

ROGER BENNETT

FINANCIAL TIMES MANAGEMENT
128 Long Acre, London WC2E 9AN
Tel: +44 (0)171 447 2000
Fax: +44 (0)171 240 5771
Website: www.ftmanagement.com

A Division of Financial Times Professional Limited

First published in Great Britain 1989
This edition published in Great Britain in 1998

© Financial Times Professional Limited 1998

The right of Roger Bennett to be identified as
Author of this Work has been asserted by him in accordance
with the Copyright, Designs and Patents Act 1988.

ISBN 0 273 63565 4

British Library Cataloguing in Publication Data
A CIP catalogue record for this book can be obtained from the British Library.

10 9 8 7 6 5 4 3 2 1

Typeset by Northern Phototypesetting Co. Ltd, Bolton
Printed and bound in Great Britain by Bell & Bain Ltd, Glasgow

The Publishers' policy is to use paper manufactured from sustainable forests.

About the Author

Roger Bennett has many years' experience of helping small businesses to improve their profitability. His past career has included ten years in management consultancy plus periods in the mining and metallurgical industries, and with a leading UK commercial bank. Roger's current interests are in the field of exporting and, in particular, export management for small firms. He also writes extensively on small businesses and general management topics and is the author of many books and a large number of articles on various aspects of marketing and business management.

Contents

Contents

Preface

Many small firms and SMEs that go under do so not because they are worthless businesses, but simply because their owners do not bother to rethink their basic aims and policies when profits begin to fall. Often, these businesses are fundamentally sound, and can be saved if only the people in charge devise and implement a handful of straightforward strategies for turning their firms around.

It was the sight of so many hard-working small business and SME owners failing to achieve the results their efforts objectively deserved that prompted me to write this book. So often it is the case that their real problems actually lie more in bad attitudes towards detailed day-to-day procedures than in particular inadequacies of marketing, personnel, organisation or control. Time and again I find that a change in attitude is all that is necessary to correct the situation.

The concepts discussed in the following chapters are not difficult to understand, but they do require fresh approaches to how you think about your business. Frequently, low-profit firms are not inefficient or prone to extravagant spending, nor do they offer inferior or unwanted goods; it is just that they are not capable of accommodating change. They fail to take account of changing markets, new patterns of competition and/or methods of doing business, and they do not gather the information (about market opportunities, costs, customer preferences, behaviour of competitors, new production systems and so on) that are needed for survival in today's fiercely competitive environment.

In preparing the text, I have drawn on many years of personal experience of assisting small businesses and SMEs to improve their fortunes. The book tells you how to revitalise your organisation, present and promote your output effectively, tighten your systems for credit and other forms of control, and generally how to plan and prepare for change. Specifically, you will learn techniques for:

- collecting your debts quickly and efficiently, and how to take people to court if they stubbornly refuse to pay;
- cutting costs;
- rationalising your workforce and dealing with unproductive employees;
- locating and penetrating new markets.

Additionally, the book contains useful advice on dealing with troublesome creditors and, for the business in very serious financial difficulty, I explain the extent of the personal liability of a small business or SME owner in the unfortunate event of their business collapsing.

This is a practical book, intended to make you want to do things for yourself rather than simply sit back and rely on expensive outside advice – which you can't really afford and which might not be appropriate to the needs of your firm. In business, you have to make things happen rather than just hang around waiting for events. Accordingly, positive strategies for diversifying, advertising, repositioning products and segmenting markets are suggested, based on your willingness to do these things yourself without forever seeking external assistance. There are, I believe, ideas within the following chapters capable of improving the profitability of every small business or SME.

I assume you own the firm, have been established for anything up to five years, and only employ a small number of people. You are solvent, but feel that the business is generating a lower return than is possible, and that the profits you achieve do not reflect the objective worth of the enterprise. For convenience, I commonly refer to businesses that supply 'goods', but this in no way implies that most of the ideas suggested do not apply equally to service firms, including professional and consultancy businesses.

Roger Bennett

Where is your business headed?

1

Introduction

Myths and realities about small business and
    SME management

Analysing problems

What are your business' strengths?

Your personal strengths and weaknesses

Problems beyond your control

Where do you need to be? • New products or services

The way ahead • Summary • Checklist

INTRODUCTION

Too many small firms collapse within a few years, sometimes just a few months, of starting up. Yet many of these businesses could have been saved if only their owners had spotted the first signs of serious trouble at an early stage and acted to eliminate them. Do not be intimidated by the reality of high rates of small business and SME failure (about 85 per cent of all new businesses go under within five years of their inception), but do recognise that all businesses have to overcome real problems in order to avoid failure in the early stages. Only then can long-term success be achieved.

My purpose in writing this book is to encourage you to think creatively and, above all, adventurously about the structure and operations of your business: how you run it, the scope and variety of its activities, its organisation, administration and how you present the business and its products to outsiders. There are numerous ways in which the efficiency and profitability of a small firm may be increased, and even if your business is presently experiencing severe problems, there is still an enormous amount you can do to improve its fortunes.

MYTHS AND REALITIES ABOUT SMALL BUSINESS AND SME MANAGEMENT

People who have never done it themselves cannot fully appreciate the problems attached to running your own firm. Friends and relatives naively assume that because you own a business you:

- are loaded with money;
- spend most of your time on holiday;
- do little more (when you do occasionally visit the premises) than give orders to employees who, in fact, do most of the work!

Outsiders are often blissfully unaware of how much effort you actually put into building up the firm. They forget how you worked in the evenings, at weekends and on bank holidays and how you still thought constantly about the business on your 'days off'!

However, no matter how industrious, thrifty and self-disciplined you are, you might still have a firm that is underperforming, and the realisation that the enterprise isn't earning you a proper living can be profoundly worrying.

■ Where is your business headed?

Do not be too disappointed if these comments sound disagreeably familiar: low productivity is not unusual in small and SME firms and if your last quarter's returns were poor, you are not alone. Yet, no matter how bleak your current prospects appear, there are still numerous measures you can initiate to increase your profitability. Many people have been down this road before you. They have confronted the sources of underperformance in their businesses, and have ended up with highly successful enterprises at their journey's end. The fact that you are reading this book proves you are serious about improving the business and ensuring its long-term survival.

■ Be realistic about your prospects

When you launched your firm you probably read one of the innumerable books currently available on how to set up and run a small business. Some of these texts are excessively – even childishly – optimistic and either omit all reference to the stark and sometimes unpleasant realities of potential business collapse, or fail to discuss them adequately. They do not tell you about the real problems of small business management – unpaid debts, angry creditors, threats of legal action, lazy and incompetent employees, the loss of important customers, insurance policies that turn out to be useless, inadequate premises, rent reviews that cripple your operations and so on.

Possibly you initiated the enterprise at a time that, with the benefit of hindsight, guaranteed it could not be wholly successful (especially if, like so many new businesses, you started up following widespread local redundancies and, hence, local economic recession). Now, you have to fundamentally rethink the entire situation and analyse, honestly and comprehensively, your firm's weaknesses and your personal contributions to its inadequacies.

ANALYSING PROBLEMS

A small handful of key variables consistently cause businesses to falter. Your business might:

- be in the wrong place;
- offer the wrong product to the market;
- collect and base decisions on the wrong information;
- employ the wrong people;
- be too lax in controlling the credit allowed to customers;
- cost too much, unnecessarily, to operate.

Associated with these central difficulties is a whole series of other troublesome issues resulting, perhaps, in shortages of cash, over-investment in land, buildings, machinery, furniture and so on (fixed assets), excessively high levels of working capital (money needed to operate the business from day to day), poor orga-nisation and inefficient utilisation of staff. Later chapters will help you identify these problems within your firm and suggest practical measures for dealing with them. Much of what follows is based on the idea of management auditing – namely, the application of systematic and analytical procedures to help you establish:

> Establish:
> where your business is now;
> where it needs to be in the future;
> what you have to do to get it there.

- where your business is now;
- where it needs to be in the future;
- what you have to do to get it there.

■ Important questions

Ask yourself the following questions.

■ *Why did I start the business, and am I actually doing now what I originally planned?*

If you are, in fact, undertaking the lines of work you first intended, but are still not earning a living, then you probably need to reposi-tion the business *vis-à-vis* its actual and potential markets. Perhaps you didn't appreciate how hard it would be to market your product. You thus altered its design and presentation to make it easier to sell, but, in doing this, you may have lost your direction and wandered into areas in which the firm is inexperienced. Later on in the book I will tell you how to 'segment' your markets so that you can then target your selling efforts more effectively.

■ Can I calculate the following information quickly and accurately?

- How long, on average, does it take to collect an outstanding debt?
- The average periods that stocks of the things I buy from outside stand idle before they are used and stocks of finished goods stay on the premises awaiting despatch?
- Average stockholding costs?
- How long elapses, on average, before I pay my bills?
- What rates of return am I obtaining on each of the activities undertaken?
- How long, on average, does it take me to issue invoices?
- What is the likely effect on sales and revenues of my offering a small discount for prompt settlement of accounts?
- Which of my products are the slowest moving?
- Which products contribute most to aggregate profits and why?
- Is the product with the highest profit mark-up on cost the best-selling of the firm's products, and if not why not?
- When did each of my main competitors last change their prices ?
- How many methods of distribution other than those I use at present are available to me?

If you cannot answer these questions fairly easily, there is probably something wrong with your information-gathering system. How this can be improved is explained later in the chapter.

■ Is work duplicated within the business, and how can costs be reduced?

Few people fully appreciate the extent of the hidden costs of running a small business or SME. You must be totally ruthless when curbing unnecessary expenditure. Chapter 4 offers suggestions for how day-to-day efficiency may be improved. Heed these carefully as no private-sector business can possibly survive in the long term if its day-to-day methods of operation are inefficient.

WHAT ARE YOUR BUSINESS' STRENGTHS?

Next, analyse the strengths and weaknesses of the enterprise, focusing on what the business is really good at and where its performance might be improved. Answer the following questions.

- What are the major selling points of each product or service and why should anyone buy from you and not another firm?
- How are your personal relationships with suppliers, employees and your bank?
- Is your equipment up to date or does much of it need replacing?
- Which three improvements in your administrative organisation would you most like to see?
- How long into the future can you reasonably expect your existing products to sell without having to alter their design or contents?
- How often do you receive customer complaints, and have you ever sat back and really analysed why your customers have complained?
- What sort of image of your business do you think your premises, stationery and letterheads project to the outside world?

YOUR PERSONAL STRENGTHS AND WEAKNESSES

You should by now be starting to formulate a critical and objective overview of the business' current situation. Analyse your competences. Did you establish the business without possessing sufficient resources or business or technical expertise? Do you lack communications skills, evidenced perhaps by your reluctance to enter into business correspondence, use the phone or by an inability to 'connect' with others on a personal level? You will find advice on interpersonal communication skills in various situations in later chapters.

PROBLEMS BEYOND YOUR CONTROL

Of course, certain problems originate externally and are thus beyond your control, such as:

- undercutting by competitors;
- unforeseeable changes in public taste;
- tax, rates and interest rate increases;
- economic depressions;
- technological innovations.

However, you should still be able to study and quickly identify these events – if you cannot, there is probably something wrong. Later on in the book I will explore how you might

In short, you will see how to make things happen rather than merely sitting back and waiting for external events to sink your business.

identify and develop new market opportunities and technical innovations, how you can spot inefficiencies and reduce expenditure, revise your scale of operations and rationalise your product range. In short, you will see how to make things happen rather than merely sitting back and waiting for external events to sink your business.

WHERE DO YOU NEED TO BE?

Total reliance on a single product, or selling several products but only to one market, invites difficulties for your firm. So many things can go wrong:

- a change in fashion;
- sharp seasonal variations in demand;
- reduced consumer incomes in the single market serviced;
- competitors' actions;
- unexpected rises in raw materials and other input prices;
- VAT increases and so on.

Not only does a single-product policy leave you vulnerable to changes in market conditions, it also creates rigidities in your production, organisation and distribution systems. Your plant and equipment becomes increasingly specialised, so that it cannot be used for other purposes when business is slack. Also, its resale value will be negligible if there is widespread depression in the industry to which the assets relate. Your staff, moreover, become completely attuned to the processes and skill requirements of a single product and supply system and so become unable or unwilling to undertake other, unfamiliar activities and routines. Even if your single-product/single-market policy is brilliantly successful, the time will come when your existing market is so saturated that no further sales increases can occur.

Ideally, you should have a variety of customers across many different places or industries (so that a depression in a single place or industry does not hit you too hard) and will offer differing credit terms to various categories of customers according to their importance, reliability and how quickly they settle their bills.

■ Think about the possibilities for diversification

Ideally, you should have a variety of customers across many different places or industries (so that a depression in a single place or industry does not hit you too hard) and will offer differing credit terms to various categories of customers according to their importance, reliability and how quickly they settle their bills. Diversification across markets is also useful for a small firm or SME that has already captured a large part – perhaps the dominant part – of a small market segment that rivals have overlooked. To increase market share from 85 per cent to 90 per cent of an existing market segment is considerably more difficult than increasing from a 3 per cent share to a 15 per cent share of an entirely new one. Good credit control is essential if you are to diversify your credit arrangements, and advice on this is offered in Chapter 5.

■ Could you diversify?

Even if you are extremely good at what you are currently doing and operate within a seemingly stable industry, you still need to look out for profitable diversification opportunities. Indeed, your only hope of survival in the long term may depend on your ability to introduce profitable new lines. Products and services can be defined as much by the manner in which they are sold and presented as by their physical characteristics. Thus, a change in selling methods, say by:

- introducing direct mail ordering;
- offering cash and carry facilities;
- creating a new package design;
- making easy payment terms available and so on;

can be a form of product diversification in itself as, indeed, are changes in:

- quality
- colour
- layout of operating instructions
- the literature that accompanies your product.

All of these moves can redefine and/or reposition your output in your customers' minds.

Markets change continuously, and you need to be able to identify and seize opportunities as they arise. This means you have to be able to spot chances quickly and gather just the right sorts of information.

■ Information

An effective information-gathering system enables you to watch all your costs and revenues carefully; identify possibilities for improving efficiency, introducing profitable new products and entering new markets; and to search the wider business environment for developments of interest to your firm. It provides the information necessary for day-to-day control (ratios of stock to output, profit to working capital and so on) and, importantly, generates data on changes in the long-term efficiency of your various operations and, hence, whether or not you need to abandon current activities in favour of alternative opportunities.

> *Markets change continuously, and you need to be able to identify and seize opportunities as they arise. This means you have to be able to spot chances quickly and gather just the right sorts of information.*

You must monitor rates of return on capital employed (see Chapter 3), cash flows, the firm's liquidity position and the performances of specific investment projects. Accurate marketing information is crucial to the success of your firm. This should include data on:

- the effectiveness of advertising;
- responsiveness of sales to price changes;
- behaviour of competitors;
- the efficiency of distributors;
- lengths of trading cycles (that is, the periods that elapse between making a product and its sale to the final consumer);
- trends in various market segments;
- frequency and causes of stockouts, the identification of slow-moving items and stockholding costs.

Another essential duty is to highlight potential problems with debtors and suppliers. Your system should be capable of answering the following questions.

- What is the average delay between delivery of goods or performance of service and the issuing of invoices?
- How quickly do customers settle their accounts?
- What are the effects of offering discounts for prompt payment?
- What is the ratio of creditors to purchasers?
- How long, on average, do suppliers take to deliver goods?
- To what extent can payments to suppliers be delayed?

NEW PRODUCTS OR SERVICES

If the information generated suggests you are in the wrong business, you need to look around for new products and services. Either you must think up completely different products or copy (taking care not to breach other firms' patents and trademarks) someone else's products while altering a few of their features. (Actually, attempts at imitating other products may themselves create the inspiration necessary to invent something entirely new.)

Write out lists of all the types of work your firm is competent to undertake and of all the alternatives to your product that exist or are feasible. Can you change the product's shape, size, contents, colour or structure? How do foreign versions of the product differ from yours? If you don't know how foreigners make or present this type of good, ask your local Chamber of Commerce to suggest some foreign magazines that might illustrate overseas firms' approaches to the design and supply of this kind of product.

■ The small firm's or SME's advantage

Small firms and SMEs frequently enjoy an advantage over larger rivals in the introduction of new products. Typically they:

- are more flexible;
- do not have large amounts of capital locked into particular technologies or distribution networks and may thus be better equipped to respond quickly to fresh market opportunities.

Can you diversify into products related to those you already supply? Do your own suppliers or end customers do things that you might be able to do better? Ask your major suppliers and customers whether or not they have product needs that they experience difficulty in fulfilling. Even customer complaints can generate new ideas for products!

■ Introducing products

Having listed some possible new products you next have to examine their technical, marketing, and production cost feasibilities critically. Analyse the supply costs of the various options and assess the profitability of each alternative. Look in particular at:

- how many customers are likely to buy the intended new product;
- where potential consumers are located and precisely why they should want to buy the item;
- to what extent the intended product will enhance your business' image – if it will cause you to appear conventional and old-fashioned or make you seem innovative and up to date;
- how you expect market demand for the new product to develop and what the cash flow implications of the forecast pattern of sales are.

Once you are happy about these matters, you need to check to ensure that the product embodies selling points that will appeal to customers, that it will perform satisfactorily under normal conditions and that it is safe in storage and use. Now you can draft a timetable for introducing the product, bearing in mind that if the launch is successful, competition will quickly and inevitably emerge.

■ When to withdraw a product

Many businesses fail because they do not phase out old products as new ones are introduced. This results in:

- complicated and expensive production and organisation systems;
- several independent production processes;
- many varieties of raw materials drawn from several different sources;
- non-interchangeable components and spare parts;
- differing customer types (and, hence, the need for different advertising messages and media) and so on.

Rationalisation and standardisation of the product range may offer substantial cost savings, so existing products should be withdrawn as soon as their production and sale ceases to be financially worth while.

Products can be likened to people – they are conceived, born, mature and die. The impending demise of a product might be evidenced by declining sales and unit profitability, and by an increase in the amount of effort needed to achieve the lower level of sales. It may be worth while cutting the product price – perhaps in combination with a special promotion (a coupon offer, for example) – just to see what happens. If the response is poor, the product should be phased out. Otherwise, increasing amounts of time, effort, money and other resources will be devoted to maintaining a product that is coming to the end of its natural life.

THE WAY AHEAD

So overwhelming might the problems outlined in previous sections appear that you are beginning to wonder whether or not you really want to continue the business. What are the alternatives? Can you get a steady job if the business collapses? There is no point ruining your health or peace of mind merely to struggle on with a no-hope enterprise. If you decide there is absolutely no chance of the firm succeeding (especially if you cannot even cover the fixed costs – rent, rates, heating and lighting and so on – of the establishment), then you should immediately cancel any orders on the books that will not generate profit and do not carry a prohibitive cancellation penalty (though payment of a small penalty may in fact, be financially worth while) and start to wind up your operation. If, conversely, you do decide to carry on – and I hope for your sake that this option exists – then you must recognise and accept that drastic, possibly ruthless, turnaround measures may be necessary. You might have to make loyal and hard-working employees redundant, and you will almost certainly need to redirect the fundamental orientation of the firm and radically alter its working methods. The steps involved are as follows:

- conduct a searching analysis of your individual and of your firm's strengths and weaknesses;
- establish a skeleton staff of totally flexible employees to implement crisis measures;
- put an immediate embargo on all new capital expenditures and introduce a programme for significantly reducing the costs of operations, linking all expenditures to immediately identifiable short-term benefits;
- tighten credit control procedures and seek emergency sources of finance to inject into the firm;
- prepare emergency cash flow forecasts to pinpoint critical dangers and activities;
- reorganise the firm's administrative structure and, simultaneously, redefine its target market segments, advertising strategy and sales promotions methods;

- smarten your business' image, revise its price structure and carefully examine the adequacy of your present selling and distribution systems.

You also need to ask whether or not you really need your existing premises. These issues are explored in subsequent chapters.

SUMMARY

Many firms experience low rates of return, but there is much that can be done quickly and easily to improve a small business' or SME's fortunes. You must not be discouraged by the fact that your firm is not as profitable as you first expected, and it is essential that you adopt an innovative and creative approach to the business' future.

In fact, a handful of key problems consistently cause underperformance in small firms and SMEs, so provided you:

- know what these are;
- can identify them swiftly;
- stand ready to implement decisive policies for overcoming immediate crises;

your profits should improve.

Think of your firm as a system, with inputs of labour and materials and so on, and outputs of finished goods and/or services. The business exists to convert these inputs into outputs and then distribute the resulting products. This involves deciding what lines of work the firm should undertake and doing the work as efficiently as possible. In determining these matters, you must consider:

- your product's present and potential positions *vis-à-vis* various market segments;
- the strengths and weaknesses of the firm, its opportunities for development and the external threats it faces.

Relying on a single product or market invites trouble. You should actively seek to diversify your output and market coverage. Markets change continuously and you have to be able to grasp opportunities immediately they become available. This means searching for new products, carefully analysing the profitabilities of existing output and withdrawing existing products before they become a financial liability. Sound information systems are thus vitally important for the long-term survival of the business.

To revitalise the firm, you will probably have to reorganise its administrative structure, redefine its markets and marketing objectives, tighten its procedures for credit control and introduce new and better advertising, sales promotions and other marketing policies.

✓ Checklist

☐ How do your firm's current operations compare with those you originally intended when you started the business? How do you explain differences?

☐ What is your actual rate of profit compared to the rate of profit you predicted when you began operations?

☐ Did you start the business when local economic conditions were not conducive to its survival and, if so, how have the effects of local economic recession affected the business' performance?

☐ What outstanding difficulties have you experienced since starting up? Are these difficulties the ones you most expected when you began the business?

☐ How quickly and accurately can you identify trading and other business problems when they arise?

☐ Which inputs (of labour, raw materials, components and so on) have caused you most difficulties and why?

☐ Which aspects of your firm's operations have been most successful and why?

☐ Do you feel technically competent to deal with the new products you have introduced and/or new markets you have recently entered? How might you obtain training to help you cope with these matters?

☐ How long would it take you to find out:
  – the weekly cost of holding one unit of stock;
  – how long, on average, it takes to collect outstanding debts;

       – the average period that elapses between your receiving suppliers' invoices and settling the amounts owed?

☐ How many new products might it be feasible for your business to introduce over the next three years?

☐ What are the essential features that differentiate your product from that of competing firms?

☐ What is the average length of your trading cycle?

☐ How recently did you examine the efficiency of your distribution system? If the answer to this question is 'A long time ago', why have you neglected this vital aspect of your operations?

Troubleshooting

Introduction • Do-it-yourself management consultancy
What you need to study • The business environment
Cash flow problems • Breaking even
Causes and consequences of bad management
Summary • Checklist

INTRODUCTION

When you are ill and go to the doctor, you expect the doctor to diagnose the cause of your ailment. They will ask a series of questions and, from the answers, conclude why it is you are feeling unwell. Doctors normally apply one of two approaches to diagnosis – inductive or deductive – depending on the available information and the seriousness of the complaint.

The deductive approach involves asking general questions first and then narrowing down the range of possible origins of the problem as the consultation proceeds. Questions become increasingly specific until the reason for your illness is discovered. There are two difficulties with deductive questioning. These are the vast range of questions that might be asked and the fact that asking a particular question can put an idea into the patient's mind. For example, people who are asked if they have been having headaches may suddenly decide that they have, even if this is not actually the case.

Inductive diagnosis means the doctor takes one look at you and, from their many years' experience of treating similar illnesses, provisionally assumes a certain cause. Then you are asked questions to confirm or reject this opinion. The problem here is that the initial assessment may be incorrect so that the doctor then pursues several wild goose chases before reaching the correct diagnosis.

DO-IT-YOURSELF MANAGEMENT CONSULTANCY

Discovering what has gone wrong with a business is much the same as a visit to your doctor. You may inwardly feel that you know the source of poor performance, yet be unable to establish conclusively the cause of the complaint. Typically, you need to begin the investigation with a general assessment of all aspects of the operations of the business and then narrow down the list of things that might have gone wrong. A good management consultant would guide you in these respects, but you may not be able to afford outside advice and so must do this work independently (and, anyhow, the work is interesting).

Imagine you are an outsider brought in to analyse the efficiency of your firm. You must be objective, rational, realistic and, above all, brutally honest about the situation.

■ Cause and effect

The aim is to establish connections between causes and effects, and then to impose new management structures and patterns of interpersonal relationships (you might, for example, have previously been too soft with your debtors or employees) in order to remedy the business' faults. Then, you will be able to predict how your business responds (or should respond) to changes in the things that cause difficulties. Suppose, for instance, that you know how much your sales will probably increase if you reduce your selling price by a certain percentage, and that you have also identified the relationship between the volume of production and unit cost. You can now work out the likely consequences for production costs and schedules of an aggressive price-cutting marketing

> *One useful approach is to specify exactly what you initially wanted (and still hope to achieve) from the business and then work back through your entire organisation, highlighting the inefficiencies that have prevented you achieving your objectives.*

strategy and incorporate these directly into your business plan. Ignorance costs money in the commercial world, and the resources devoted to collecting relevant information on the causes and effects of various activities are usually justified.

■ How to begin

One useful approach is to specify exactly what you initially wanted (and still hope to achieve) from the business and then work back through your entire organisation, highlighting the inefficiencies that have prevented you achieving your objectives. You then describe how your business ought to perform and compare this ideal with what actually happens.

Suppose, for example, you run a wine bar and that, when you started, you anticipated a certain average number of customers per week, each spending a particular average amount, thus generating an income of a predicted level well in excess of your anticipated costs.

19

What precisely needs to happen for this to occur? Presumably, the answer to this question will involve:

- a certain proportion of potential customers in the wine bar's catchment area becoming aware of the establishment's existence, using the establishment and repeating their custom;
- each customer unit (person or group) spending some minimum amount per standard period of time (half an hour, perhaps) while in the bar;
- a certain average hourly turnover of custom and/or seat/table occupancy;
- pay and other expenses not exceeding predetermined limits;
- a constant supply of inputs (wines, foodstuffs and so on) at reasonable prices.

The actual list will, of course, be much more exhaustive than this and relate to the specific circumstances of the business. In general, however, you would need to ask how each of your objectives could be achieved and why targets have not been met. You want to know:

- what resources, activities and other inputs are needed;
- how you and your employees must behave towards customers and towards each other;
- what information you have to gather;
- how materials are to be stored and manipulated.

Now compare the ideal configuration of events and activities with the reality of your business and determine the changes necessary to improve its performance. Some fundamental changes – in premises, marketing methods, staffing levels, ways of controlling costs – are dealt with in other chapters. Here we are concerned with identifying causes of difficulties.

WHAT YOU NEED TO STUDY

The symptoms of poor performance (declining profitability, low sales, soaring expenditures) are obvious, but their causes may be hidden. Experiments may thus be necessary to determine the sources of problems.

■ Experiments and research

You can experiment with:

- the price of your product (special price reductions, special offers and so on);
- how you package output;
- where you place advertisements;
- the allocation of tasks to various employees;
- staff incentive schemes and so on.

Normally, you would not wish to change your activities constantly, but the circumstances of a low-profit business are not normal, and your firm could fail unless drastic measures are implemented.

■ The competition

There is much wishful thinking when newly established firms evaluate the calibre of their competitors. Proprietors convince themselves of the superiority of their own businesses, to the point where they perceive competitors in a totally unrealistic manner. If your business succeeds you must expect other firms to respond aggressively – if they do not,

Look ahead. Anticipate competitors' behaviour and prepare contingency plans for dealing with various responses to your actions

you have a clear indication that you have failed to make a significant impact on chosen market segments.

Three reactions from competitors are likely:

- an increase in their advertising and other promotional activities;
- price cuts; and
- their copying your products and initiatives.

Look ahead. Anticipate competitors' behaviour and prepare contingency plans for dealing with various responses to your actions. Be prepared, too, for dirty tricks from competitors, including:

- attempts to persuade your suppliers (via financial inducements) not to accept your orders or, at least, to insist on cash payment;

- circulating unfounded rumours to your largest customers that you are on the verge of bankruptcy;
- pretending to be recruiting staff, inviting your own employees to apply for (non-existent) vacancies, and then interviewing them simply to gather information about your current operations;
- persuading retailers and/or distributors not to handle your products.

Monitor your competitors' activities continuously and never underestimate their worth. If you have employees, a good way of following competitors' actions is to make each employee personally responsible for keeping tabs on one particular competitor – by perusing their advertisements, cataloguing the selling points of their current products, watching their staffing levels, price policies and so on.

■ Beware the predatory competitor

Paradoxically, the greater your success, the greater the danger competitors can become to your long-term survival! Suppose you are so technically efficient and your advertising so effective that you now dominate the local market. At this point (supposing, for example, that you have a three-quarters share of the market), the only way you can increase your sales further is by expanding the total size of the market (a task that is both difficult and expensive). Yet, a less successful rival can increase its market share – and hence its sales – at your expense by cutting its prices and taking some of your existing custom. You have little alternative but to respond by cutting your prices. However, your own sales are unlikely to increase in consequence because you already dominate the market. Thus, you lower your prices and accept the resulting decline in profits.

Unfortunately, however, this enforced cut in revenue occurs just at the moment that funds are most needed, as in order to dominate the market in the first instance, you had to:

- invest in new equipment;
- undertake expensive advertising;
- enter high-value bulk purchasing contracts with suppliers;
- employ more staff;
- rent a warehouse to store extra goods and so on.

To finance these activities, you borrowed heavily and the loan plus interest is now due for repayment. The reduction in profits for you by a competitor's actions means you can't find the money. Your very success in outpacing competitors is thus actually causing the failure of your business!

THE BUSINESS ENVIRONMENT

The worst time to start a new business is during an economic depression when consumer incomes, and hence the general demand for products, are falling. Yet these are precisely the conditions that typically prevail when governments most vigorously encourage the establishment of new firms. Perhaps you started your enterprise during a tax regime that suddenly altered or depended on government or local authority support that unexpectedly collapsed or arrived at work one morning to find double yellow lines on the streets where previously your customers parked their vehicles. As a small business or SME, you are unlikely to experience strikes within your own organisation, but you could be affected by strikes (or other mishaps) among your suppliers, distributors or large industrial customers.

■ Plan ahead

Such difficulties arise from factors beyond your control and so you are not responsible for their consequences. However, you should plan ahead and make provision for various environmental eventualities. Planning enables you to decide today, unhurriedly, how you will react to diverse future situations. It means you do not have to make crucial decisions, which could make or break the business, in a crisis atmosphere when you do not have time to consider all the relevant facts objectively. The business that plans is ready to adapt its activities to suit altered environments and it can take action now to help it cope with possible future occurrences. Planning forces you to think hard about your organisation, its strengths and weaknesses and its future prospects. Many pitfalls might then be foreseen and thus avoided.

CASH FLOW PROBLEMS

Cash flow problems certainly make themselves known to the poorly planned small business or SME, if only because there's not enough money in the bank to settle outstanding invoices. Yet, the business might otherwise be financially viable and have excellent prospects. You must analyse how cash flow difficulties arise – it is not sufficient merely to observe that cash inflows fail to arrive in appropriate periods. Prepare lists of all your receipts and expenditures for the last six months and highlight major weekly differences. Almost certainly, you will find that inflow problems relate either to unexpected reductions in sales or to credit customers taking unacceptably long periods to settle their balances. Outflow problems are usually caused by natural (or man-made) catastrophes that could and should have been insured against or by excessive and/or unanticipated expenditures.

Predicting and monitoring cash inflows and outflows and analysing the differences between them are crucially important for the small firm or SME as failure to do this is one of the commonest causes of their collapse.

■ Planning cash flow

One way of planning cash flow is to anchor all spending against sales revenues. Hence, expenditures on anything other than current pay and production supplies are deferred until after prespecified sales revenues (not sales volume or credit) have been achieved. This is a cheap and simple control device that avoids many cash flow problems. However, it has the severe disadvantage of automatically reducing certain expenditures when perhaps they ought to increase as sales might themselves depend on various activities the funding of which is arbitrarily withdrawn just because sales are reducing. Also, you do not wish to give the appearance of being in trouble. External signs of financial problems, such as:

- failing to repaint the reception area;
- not cleaning offices or the fascia of the premises;
- continuing to run ageing and obviously unreliable vehicles and so on;

can be most damaging to the image of the business. Good-quality stationery, bold letterheads, printed (rather than typed and photo-copied) sales literature and so on can be crucial for marketing the firm. However, linking costs to sales revenue can be extremely use-ful to an enterprise facing immediate cash flow difficulties and, sen-sibly applied, it might save the business.

BREAKING EVEN

A frequent cause of cash flow problems is failure to realise the rev-enue implications of various pricing policies. Sometimes, price cuts lead to such big increases in sales that the effects of a lower price per unit are easily outweighed by the additional revenues generated by an increased volume of business. For instance, a firm selling 5000 units per quarter at £5.00 per unit realises £25,000 from sales. Suppose the firm has £10,000 per quarter in overheads (rent, rates, lighting and heating and so on) and that each unit costs £2.00 to supply. The firm is making £5000 profit per quarter. Now suppose the selling price is reduced to £4.00 per unit. This business must now sell 5000 units just to break even, let alone make any profit, and must sell 7500 units if its existing profit level of £5000 per quarter is to continue.

To see this, remember that the breakeven point occurs when total revenue equals total cost. Revenue is price times number of units sold – that is, £4.00 x X, where X is the number of units. Total cost consists of overheads of £10,000, plus cost per unit times the num-ber of units produced – that is, £2.00 x X. Thus, to break even we need:

total revenue = total cost
that is $4X = 10,000 + 2X$
so that $X = 5000$ units

To make £5000 profit, total revenue must exceed total cost by this amount, viz:

$$4X = (10,000 + 2X) + 5000$$
so that $X = 7500$ units

is the number of units required. Accordingly, you must always work out how many extra units have to be sold to make a price cut financially viable. In the example given, it might, in fact, be impossible to increase sales from 5000 to at least 7500 units. And if competitors cut their prices in response, with the result that sales do not increase at all, then all the existing profit is wiped out (£4.00 x 5000 gives £20,000), leaving just enough to break even.

Before even considering a price cut (or increase), therefore, you need to calculate an array of possible prices with their breakeven points and cost/revenue implications clearly indicated. Note that a low price associated with a high breakeven point might be appropriate for a market that is buoyant and expanding and where production costs are not likely to increase without warning, but may be totally unsuitable for other situations. A big pay increase for staff, raw materials price rises or an increase in the rent of your premises will disrupt your intended point of breakeven and, hence, all your planned production schedules.

CAUSES AND CONSEQUENCES OF BAD MANAGEMENT

Some problems might be due to your own incompetence. Face up to this – accept your past failings, but resolve never to repeat your mistakes. Common managerial indiscretions include the following.

Relying on just a couple of really big customers for most of your orders and not seeking to diversify your market can spell disaster for your firm.

■ Not enough customers

Relying on just a couple of really big customers for most of your orders and not seeking to diversify your market can spell disaster for your firm. One of these large customers might:

- decide to withdraw its business;
- go into liquidation;
- itself experience financial problems and not be able to settle the outstanding balance it has accumulated.

■ Too few suppliers

Not seeking alternative sources of supply is equally dangerous. You may perhaps have negotiated an attractive discount for bulk purchases of raw materials from a particular supplier. In doing this, however, you failed to realise the longer-term implications of relying on a single source of supply. The following difficulties might be especially severe:

- the discount might be withdrawn, by which time your production line may have been adapted to suit the specific characteristics of the output of the supplying firm;
- deliveries from the single supplier might be regularly late and cause numerous hold-ups in your manufacturing system;
- the proportion of defective items in each delivery may become unacceptably high.

Reliance on just a couple of suppliers means, moreover, that if they unexpectedly increase their prices and if you cannot easily pass on such increases (via a higher selling price) to your own customers, your profit margin is reduced – at least in the short to medium term. Also, a declining margin could mean the end of the business.

Finding alternative suppliers capable of delivering the possibly substantial amounts of raw materials you require – on time, at an acceptable level of quality and at a reasonable price – can be difficult, time-consuming and expensive. So take an interest in the technical aspects of your inputs – their origin, manufacturing processes, quality options and so on. This will not only help you improve your product, but could also enable you to identify new and better sources of supply.

■ *Staff problems*

Employing staff who are lazy, inept or dishonest (or all three) is another obvious source of trouble. If this has occurred, it is largely your fault – you ought not to have hired such people in the first instance or they should have been taken to task as soon as they began to underperform. Why did you not recognise the signs of staff dishonesty or incompetence? After all, lack of enthusiasm, refusal to cooperate or exercise initiative, conflicts and bad interpersonal relationships among employees are easily observed! An inefficient employee can be the most expensive (and damaging) resource your business ever acquires. Conversely, competent staff make enormous contributions to the well-being of the organisation. Employee relations are therefore important in even the smallest of firms.

■ Capital and current spending

Failing to distinguish between capital spending and current spending creates enormous difficulties for the hard-up firm. Too many small business and SME proprietors regard all incomes and expenditures as part of their normal monthly cash flow, regardless of the purpose to which the money is applied. Thus, for example, a firm's single delivery vehicle might be its most important, and expensive, asset, yet the business' owner may make little effort to create a reserve out of current income to replace the vehicle when it wears out.

Sometimes proprietors wrongly assume that the rate of depreciation applied to an asset on the advice of an accountant – who will select the method of depreciation that saves the maximum amount of tax – is the actual rate at which money should be put aside for the asset's replacement. For instance, at the time of writing the Inland Revenue will only allow you to depreciate a motor car by, at most, 25 per cent of its initial cost in any given year. However, how long that vehicle actually lasts depends principally on how much you use it and whether or not it is well maintained. Hence, you should put aside a reasonable amount each month to cover all foreseeable asset replacement costs, and then add a contingency allowance (say 10 per cent) for good measure. Remember, too, that maintenance costs increase sharply as assets age.

Many small businesses and SMEs have gone under when confronted with large maintenance bills or when a major capital asset unexpectedly needs replacement. Remember, too, that tangible assets are necessary to provide security for bank loans. You may be able to rent a replacement capital asset temporarily if you happen to be short of funds when your existing one fails. However, you cannot offer rented equipment as security when borrowing money.

■ Market trends

Suppose you have an excellent product – technically superb, well packaged and presented and priced reasonably. Your firm is doing what it is good at and you love the work. What, you ask, could possibly be wrong with that? Unfortunately, you may be offering for sale a product that is mechanically and functionally first rate, but which consumers increasingly do not wish to buy! Markets alter in terms of the ages, sex, income levels, geographical location and so on, of potential customers and also in relation to consumer tastes and preferences. There is little point in producing technically excellent goods that consumers are not willing to purchase. Thus, instead of simply trying to sell the goods you have already decided to make (and becoming increasingly frustrated by consumers' poor reactions), you should monitor current trends among consumers, look for new market opportunities and be prepared to diversify and/or modify your offerings to satisfy current consumer preferences.

■ Change in the environment

How long is it since you compared your own products to those of competitors, especially those relatively new to the market? List all the changes in the wider environment – laws, taxation, consumer tastes, local authority regulations, input prices, operating costs, employee relations – you can think of that might affect the business and, alongside each item, briefly outline its probable consequences. Then, consider each of your firm's activities (selling, manufacture, raising finance and so on) and ask yourself what changes are likely to occur in each area. Change is inevitable. Accept change. Look ahead and plan how to cope with its consequences.

■ Spare capacity

Carrying too much spare capacity is not uncommon among small firms and SMEs, the owners of which typically dislike being under too much pressure from production deadlines, machine time and labour utilisation constraints, lack of storage space and so on. Matching current workloads with available capacity requires careful scheduling and a great deal of effort. How much easier it is to maintain a comfortable margin of spare capacity, so that any order can be met without additional administrative work?

However, consider the real cost of surplus capacity. A machine (or person or warehouse) idle for one hour a day is costing the business 14.3 per cent of its potential contribution (assuming seven hours a day normal working). Thus, avoid spare capacity, even if tight schedules are inconvenient. As soon as spare capacity appears, consider subletting the surplus and/or cutting your prices rather than breathe a sigh of relief – spare capacity (including office space and storage facilities) is costing you money, despite its convenience. Spare capacity is a frequent symptom of unprofitable expansion, which is dealt with in Chapter 3.

■ Wasteful advertising

Failing businesses sometimes naively assume that they can turn their fortunes around by increasing expenditure on advertising. They insist that their products are excellent, and genuinely believe customers will clamour to buy these products when informed of their existence. Advertisements must be carefully targeted if their costs are to be recovered and only in exceptional circumstances should advertising be undertaken where its effectiveness cannot be measured. Advertising can be enormously expensive and wasteful of resources.

■ Discretion is sometimes better than valour

Do not take on more than you can cope with. In particular, never initiate a fight with competitors when, realistically, you stand little chance of succeeding. Large firms frequently possess substantial reserves that they can and do use to 'see off' smaller rivals that initiate price or advertising wars against them. So, avoid attacking larger competitors unless you are sure you can win or those firms attacked you first. Discretion is infinitely preferable to valour in most circumstances.

■ What about your employees?

Lack of sympathy for employees who experience personal family problems that interfere with their jobs (causing them to take time off to look after children, for example) or who have difficulty coping with the level of their work, can alienate and render unprofitable people who are fundamentally sound and possess great potential. Minor concessions such as:

- allowing flexible working hours;
- paying certain small expenses;
- consultation in decision making;

can transform the situation and cause disaffected individuals to become highly satisfied employees.

■ Further problems

Control problems often figure prominently in the case histories of businesses that experience low profitability. Thus, you might start out as a one-person operation with direct, personal and intimate knowledge of every aspect of your firm, making all decisions yourself, knowing all your major customers and suppliers by name and enjoying low overheads. Then you employ staff to liaise with outsiders. You haven't the time to supervise them closely (you are too busy building up the firm) and, anyway, it would not be proper to deny them the authority to make decisions independently. However, the staff become slipshod in their work. They upset customers, do not properly inspect suppliers' deliveries and allow overdue accounts to accumulate. The telephone isn't answered, letters leave the office with errors in them and so on. All this has happened behind your back – you have lost effective control of your business!

You must plan the development of the business. Allow for steadily increasing expenditure on overheads (extra warehousing, premises, administration) in line with the growth in sales. As your business grows, increase the frequency with which you inspect vital management information – the order book, outstanding credit, delivery periods, market share and so on. These matters are discussed in the next chapter.

SUMMARY

To be good at small business management you have to be able to diagnose accurately the basic causes of business problems, and relate such causes to their operational effects. You should set up an ideal model of how the business would function in the best possible situation and then compare this with your firm's actual performance, analysing differences as you go along. You may need to experiment and undertake considerable amounts of research prior to deciding on the measures necessary to improve profitability, but once you have chosen your actions, you must stick to your plan, implementing tough, new policies to overcome your difficulties. Beware of dirty tricks by competitors – continuously monitor their activities. List and describe current operational problems under the headings:

- those created by outside influences;
- those subject to your personal and immediate control.

Be totally honest in your analysis.

Planning is essential for successful small business and SME management, particularly regarding the timing of receipts and payments. You need a system for relating current levels of spending to some measure of the business' overall performance. You must carefully examine the breakeven and cash flow implications of various selling prices.

Prosperous firms are usually those that, in the longer term, avoid overreliance on just a handful of customers or suppliers. They regularly seek out fresh markets and new sources of supply. The chapter concluded with a brief description of some of the many things that can go wrong in a small business, citing particular instances of bad management and their effects. Later chapters suggest solutions for many of these difficulties.

☑ Checklist

☐ Can you pinpoint at least four specific reasons for your profits not being as good as expected?

☐ By how much do you think your total profits would increase if you cut all selling prices by
   - 5 per cent;
   - 10 per cent;
   - 15 per cent?

☐ What are the revenue implications of the answers to the last question?

☐ How well equipped is your business to adapt quickly to the following:
   - an increase in the rate of VAT on your output;
   - a big price cut by a major competitor;
   - a strike among the employees of the firms that deliver your most important supplies?

☐ When did you last prepare a cash flow forecast?

☐ Suppose your three major suppliers increased their sale prices by 10 per cent, how would this affect the profitability of your business?

☐ How much do you know about the technical aspects of the firm's raw material inputs?

☐ Do you really understand the difference between capital spending and current spending?

☐ What is the probability that you will not experience an equipment breakdown within the next three months, and how would a serious equipment failure affect your cash flow?

☐ Do you carry spare capacity, and, if so, how much is it costing you?

Sensible expansion

INTRODUCTION

Some seemingly successful small firms expand so rapidly that they
run into all sorts of administrative and financial difficulties that,
paradoxically, cause their average unit profitability – the average
return achieved on each pound invested in a business – to be lower
than before the expansion occurred. Whereas prior to the expansion the enterprise might have obtained an average return of, say,
15 per cent on capital employed (measured, perhaps by fixed assets
plus working capital – see below), after the expansion the percentage average rate achieved may be only 10!

Disorganised and unprofitable expansion frequently causes serious financial difficulty in small businesses and SMEs, and disor-
derly and unplanned growth should be avoided at all times. Indeed,
it has led to the collapse of many firms.

To prevent haphazard expansion and the problems it creates,
you need first to understand how unprofitable growth arises and
second, to be able to identify possible sources of 'overtrading'
within your firm. Then, if you are, in fact, growing too rapidly for
your own good, you must seek ways to reduce your scale of operations sensibly.

WHY EXPANSION DOESN'T ALWAYS INCREASE PROFITABILITY

You start a new business, and it flourishes. Order books are full,
sales expand. Everyone agrees you have a reasonably priced, first-
class product that satisfies a consumer need. Your staff are hard-
working and enthusiastic, customers are delighted with the goods
you produce. Accordingly, you start to expand the scale of your
decidedly successful operations. This, alas, might be the worst thing
you could possibly do because rapid growth typically means disturbing a highly efficient existing administrative system (it must be
efficient, otherwise the firm would not have achieved the success
that caused it to expand). Also, you incur numerous unforeseen
expenses and encounter many unanticipated organisational difficulties during the expansion. To produce the extra goods needed to satisfy the increasing volume of sales, you have to spend extra money,

now, on such things as:

- additional supplies;
- more staff pay;
- higher electricity bills to run even more machines;
- extra stationery;

but you do not receive any more income from additional production until some considerable time in the future, after the goods have been sold.

■ Credit problems

Usually, a growth in sales is accompanied by an increase in the amount of credit you give to existing (and possibly new) customers, so the period between incurring expenses and collecting the money from the sale of your goods becomes very long. Moreover, the number of bad debts you incur (that is, debts for which the likelihood of the debtor paying up is so remote that all hope of retrieving the money has to be abandoned) begins to increase.

You will probably have to borrow at high interest levels to finance the gap between the additional spending on extra labour and supplies and the receipt of income from extra sales. Also, you may have over-invested in fixed assets to cope with the expansion.

■ Wasted space

Perhaps you increased the size of your premises in order to house the additional staff you hired and to provide more warehousing space and access to new machinery. Whereas previously you fully utilised every spare scrap of space in your premises – with people almost on top of each other and boxes of goods in every available corner awaiting despatch – you now have plenty of space. However, this necessarily means you are now paying money for space on which there is zero return. If you pay £10 per square foot annual rental, then every square foot of space not used represents an extra £10 per annum invested in the business without that money generating any profits at all, which means that the average return on each square foot of premises rented quickly begins to fall.

37

■ Parkinson's law begins to apply

Similar considerations apply to machines and labour. Suppose, for example, that previously you had three employees – all of whom worked extremely hard and were fully utilised throughout all seven hours of their working day. However, in order to satisfy increased consumer demand, you have now increased your labour force to six. This solves the production/clerical work problems caused by expansion, but could mean that, by easing the pressure on labour, you now have six workers each only fully employed, on average, for just five hours of each working day. 'Parkinson's law' begins to operate – work quickly expands to fill up the time made available for its completion and, in consequence, the average return on the pay for each employee (assuming you pay a flat rate weekly or monthly) goes down. Likewise with machines. Before, you had three machines constantly in operation. Now you have five, but each is only used for part of the day. Again, the average rate of return on each pound invested in machinery will decline.

■ Supply problems

While the average returns on your investments in inputs are falling, your average costs of operating the business are going up. Suppliers might not be prepared to grant credit on really big orders because the risk to them of your default is too great. Accordingly, whereas previously perhaps three-quarters of your supplies were purchased on credit (meaning, in effect, that suppliers are lending you interest-free funds), you find that after the expansion possibly fewer than half of your much bigger total purchases are on credit terms. Most supplies now have to be paid for in cash, which you draw from the large overdraft you operate at enormous interest cost. Moreover, your existing suppliers might not have been able to satisfy your increasing demands, so that you went to new and different suppliers whose deliveries in fact turned out to be extremely slow, and a lot of the goods were defective and had to be returned.

■ More clerical work

Extra staff not only mean a higher pay bill but also more employer's National Insurance contributions and additional clerical work for you in working out their PAYE. Controlling the staff becomes more difficult, especially if recently recruited staff are not familiar with the firm's line of work. You might not be skilled or experienced in staff management and thus find that employee relations problems come to dominate your working life. Administrative overheads can increase alarmingly after hiring additional staff. More space and desks are needed, more stationery is required and the expansion in the firm's general operations creates the need for more letters to customers and suppliers, extra photocopying, more printing, typing, internal memoranda, coordination meetings and so on. Also, of course, opportunities for staff malingering -- indeed, for employee fraud, theft and petty dishonesty -- expand as the workforce increases in size.

DISTRIBUTION MATTERS

Higher sales may require that you augment or change your existing distribution system. Yet, in so doing, you might lose effective control over how your goods are sold. Increased production means that someone, somewhere, has to carry extra stock. Stockholding is expensive, as goods must be:

- warehoused
- recorded
- packaged to avoid natural wastage and pilfering
- monitored and moved in and out of stores.

Also, stock is an idle asset -- money tied up in stock could be used to earn interest or, even better, generate further profits for the firm.

■ Using a wholesaler

You can, of course, pass on the cost of stockholding to a wholesaler who will also bear the risk of collapse in sales. Unfortunately, wholesalers demand big discounts on bulk purchases – discounts so big that use of a wholesaler might not be financially worth while – and they typically stock competing brands, so there is no reason for them to promote your product rather than the output of competing firms.

Conversely, you might decide to retail your own products, acquiring retail premises for this purpose. In this case, however, you have to incur even more fixed costs and will probably need to borrow very heavily, at high interest, to finance the deal. Also, you must assume all retailing risks.

Many businesses fail as a result of taking on these sorts of retail distribution obligations without properly considering the extra work involved or the additional expertise and business experience required.

■ Small versus large orders

Distribution costs are affected by the sizes of orders that customers place (an increased volume of low-unit sales can greatly increase distribution costs as a result of increased expenditure on packaging, order processing, invoicing, debt collection and so on) and the costs of selling:

■ sales people's pay and expenses;
■ increasing travel costs as more sales staff cover bigger territories and so on.

These costs may, of course, be avoided by concentrating on selling to just a handful of really big customers. You might, for example, produce an 'own label' version of your product for a large multiple retailer or place the bulk of your output with a couple of wholesalers. However, what happens if one of these customers (which might take as much as 50 per cent of your production) decides to take its custom elsewhere or squeezes you for extra discounts or goes into liquidation owing a huge bill? You are likely to go bust as much of your productive capacity will be geared to the needs of that customer and you will probably not be able to sell this output elsewhere.

CONSEQUENCES OF EXPANDING TOO RAPIDLY

■ Increase in competition

Apart from disturbing existing production systems and possibly upsetting well-established personal relationships within the firm, a conspicuous expansion will itself signal to competitors your business' success and the fact that you are engaged in a highly profitable field. This can lead to disaster, because:

- your existing competitors might decide to expand their operations;
- other firms not presently engaged in your line of work may decide – following your profitable example – to enter your area or industry and begin to compete!

Also, the increased competition can occur precisely when you are at your most vulnerable – when you have borrowed heavily, have just paid out large amounts of cash for additional labour and raw materials and, possibly, are experiencing acute cash flow problems for the first time.

PROBLEMS WITH ADMINISTRATION AND FINANCE

Common difficulties include the following.

- Deliveries to customers are frequently late on account of the administrative problems caused by the firm's fast growth and the production bottlenecks and distribution breakdowns that are increasingly encountered.
- Debtors are slow in paying bills, excusing themselves by pointing out deficiencies in your own clerical system – your invoices miss customers' end-of-month cheque issues; invoices, delivery and advice notes sometimes conflict and are regularly inaccurate.
- It takes so long to settle these problems that you are constantly short of cash. Liabilities increase, current income falls, you have exhausted your financial reserves on the purchase of new equipment, while much of the firm's working capital is tied up in stock and in unpaid debtors' bills. You find it difficult to put together

enough money to pay your own creditors, payments to creditors are delayed for several weeks, resulting in creditors threatening to withdraw credit facilities (hence creating even more cash flow problems for the firm).

Owners of firms in this situation are sometimes incredulous about what is happening to them. They cannot believe that cash flow problems are occurring, given that the business to date has been a huge success. After all, increasing sales and, hence, the prospects for higher profits were the original impetus to expand.

> *The total amount of profit generated by higher sales continues to increase, but if you divide this by the value of the resources used to create the higher profit, you find that the average profitability of each pound invested in the business is actually lower than it was before.*

The mistake made here is to confuse absolute cash inflows with profit per unit of resource employed within the firm. True, the total amount of profit generated by higher sales continues to increase, but if you divide this by the value of the resources used to create the higher profit, you find that the average profitability of each pound invested in the business is actually lower than it was before.

■ Identify the problem

You need to compare a few key statistics before and after expansion.

A good starting point is to measure your 'rate of return on capital employed'. This is defined as profit earned during a period – say, three months – divided by the value of tangible fixed assets (plant and equipment, premises if you own them, vehicles, furniture and so on, but not including goodwill) plus current assets (stock, debtors and cash) minus current liabilities (short-term debts that have to be settled in the next six months).

If you are expanding sensibly, this ratio should not decline in value over time. Measure your profits as net profits before drawings, tax, loan repayments and the payment of interest on loans (as obviously some interest costs have to be incurred in order to finance the expansion, and such loans should not therefore be classed as part of your normal operations). Stock should be valued at cost or market value, whichever is lower. Also always deduct probable bad debts from the figure for debtors in current assets.

Valuation of fixed assets presents a problem, because of the need to deduct depreciation for wear and tear. Note that you do not have to use the same depreciation method for this purpose as you employ to save the maximum amount of tax, so choose a sensible figure that reasonably reflects the loss in asset values over the period considered.

BUSINESS RATIOS

If the rate of return on capital employed begins to decline, you must investigate the cause. Look at movements in ratios:

- for profit to sales – showing whether or not extra sales are really contributing to unit profitability;
- for sales to capital employed – which tells you how much you have to invest to generate extra sales;
- any other ratio that might be relevant for measuring your firm's efficiency – such as profit/working capital (where working capital equals current assets less current liabilities); sales to fixed assets; sales to working capital; debtors to working capital; sales to overheads; and so on.

Crucially important for effective financial control is the ratio of the firm's current assets to current liabilities.

■ The current ratio

Crucially important for effective financial control is the ratio of the firm's current assets to current liabilities. This is called the 'current ratio' (or sometimes the 'working capital ratio') of the enterprise. It shows the degree of liquidity of the business – that is, how easily the firm can (theoretically) settle its debts if all outstanding balances must be simultaneously cleared ('theoretically' because working capital includes debtors and, of course, some customers might not actually pay their bills!) Current assets of cash, debtors and stock are or should be immediately and easily converted into purchasing power, while current liabilities (trade creditors and accrued expenses) are debts that might have to be settled at short notice and, hence, drain the business of short-term funds. Also, even if you measure stock at the lower of cost or market value, there is still no guarantee that, in a real emergency, all your stock on hand could be sold. Leaving this aside, a value for this ratio of more than one means the firm is, in principle, fully solvent and can settle all its short-term debts from its own resources. Note that a current ratio of less than one is not necessarily bad – it could simply indicate that the business is economising on stocks, debtors and cash while maximising the period over which it settles its own debts. This might be suitable for a firm in a stable commercial environment where volatile change is unlikely; fixed assets could perhaps be liquidated in an emergency.

In general, however, a decreasing current ratio between one period and the next often indicates 'overtrading'. Expansion has been so fast that the growth of short-term liabilities has exceeded the accumulation of current assets.

■ The liquidity ratio

The fact that some current assets take longer to liquidate than others gives rise to the need for a ratio that measures a firm's capacity for immediate settlement of its current liabilities. The 'acid test ratio' (also called the 'liquidity ratio' or the 'quick' ratio) achieves this objective as it incorporates only those current assets that can be instantly converted into cash. Thus, stocks of raw materials and work in progress (which take some time to liquidate) are ignored. The ratio is:

$$\frac{\text{Cash} + \text{debtors} + \text{realisable investments}}{\text{Current liabilities}}$$

A more severe version would exclude debtors on the grounds that few debtors would actually meet their obligations instantly on demand. The liquidity ratio should normally have a value near to one, meaning that current liabilities are fully covered. However, values in excess of one are undesirable because superfluous liquid funds should always be quickly reinvested in order to generate additional profits for the firm; they should not be held in the form of cash or low-yield financial investments.

Finally, you should break down the current ratio into its component parts and look carefully at alterations in such ratios as stock/current assets, debtors/current assets and so on, as the business increases its sales.

WHAT TO LOOK FOR

You need to establish whether or not you are getting the same value for money from a bigger firm as you obtained previously when output and sales were less. By continuously monitoring the quick ratio (in conjunction with detailed cash flow forecasting), you ensure that you will always be able to repay loan interest and capital sum repayments to your bank and honour your other financial obligations. Thus, you will not be forced to wind up your successful business as a result of short-term lack of funds.

Before spending an extra penny on expanding your operations, look ahead to check that every additional pound put into the business will yield the same rate of return, proportionately, as that which you have already achieved and will not reduce average profits per pound put into the business.

Before spending an extra penny on expanding your operations, look ahead to check that every additional pound put into the business will yield the same rate of return, proportionately, as that which you have already achieved and will not reduce average profits per pound put into the business.

Seek out possible inefficiencies in the use of working capital. Excessive stockholding, for example, is revealed by reductions in the 'stock turnover ratio', measured as cost of sales/average stock where 'cost of sales' is the value of opening stock plus stock purchases during the period less stock at close. The ratio shows the speed of inventory turnover. If, for instance, the accounting period is one year and the ratio has a value of two, then a unit of stock is held, on average, for six months. Values lower than two mean that stock is held longer than six months, and vice versa. (High values are appropriate only for firms that face irregular and unanticipated market demands, where sudden changes in taste can lead to heavy, unexpected sales.)

Generally, fast stock turnover is desirable because rapid transformation of stock into sales means an increase in the intensity of the trading cycle (that is, how many times goods are produced and converted into cash within any given period) and, hence, higher returns on capital employed. Usually, perishable goods have the highest turnover rates, while consumer durables and luxury goods take longer to sell. Often, there are direct relationships between profit margins and stock turnover rates. Lower selling prices, while associated with lower unit prices, might cause stock to turn over so rapidly that higher total profits eventually ensue.

The average amount of raw materials stock you carry can be reduced by buying in smaller quantities that, nevertheless, are delivered more frequently. This only works, however, if suppliers' delivery arrangements are reliable and you have alternative sources of supply available if particular orders do not turn up on time. Also, you need to balance the savings in your stockholding costs against the loss of bulk purchasing discounts that may be available on larger orders.

■ Other useful ratios

Other useful ratios are:

- profits to sales;
- administrative expenses to sales – the various categories of administrative expense (selling, secretarial, documentation and so on) might also be usefully expressed as a proportion of sales;
- credit sales to total sales.

Movements in the credit/sales ratio indicate changes in the firm's dependence on credit selling and, by implication, its sensitivity to a lengthening of the average period before debtors settle their outstanding accounts. The ratio of bad debts to sales shows the risk of selling on credit. Another ratio worth computing is that of net current assets (that is, current assets minus current liabilities) to fixed assets. This indicates the extent to which physically realisable plant and equipment, premises, vehicles and so on, are available to settle outstanding debts. A high value means there are few assets that can be sold off in the event of liquidation. You must also study several crucially important operating ratios as expansion proceeds. The most important of these for a small business that makes things are the various manufacturing and machine capacity ratios, whereas an assortment of labour and other resource utilisation ratios might be more relevant to a service firm.

■ Measuring productive efficiency

First, work out how much value is added to your raw materials inputs during the course of manufacture. This can be done by deducting:

- the costs of raw materials;
- other direct manufacturing costs – labour, machine running costs and so on;
- manufacturing overheads – such as the costs of renting those parts of the firm's premises used exclusively for manufacturing, lighting and heating costs for these areas, and so on;

from the value of sales. Then you divide this 'value added in manufacturing' figure by the current value of the assets – machines, premises, tools and so on (but not consumable items, such as oil or other supplies that go into 'direct manufacturing cost') – that are used in manufacture. If this ratio falls as your business grows, then the average return from your investments in the machines, tools, premises and so on devoted to manufacture has deteriorated. Your total sales (and profits) may have increased, but the expansion of sales has led to a decline in the efficiency with which you are using your manufacturing resources – your profitability per pound spent on manufacturing has gone down.

A simpler ratio is that of sales to assets used in manufacturing, which can be subdivided into ratios for sales divided by the various categories of manufacturing assets – value of machinery, premises and so on. Similarly, the value added in manufacture can be divided in turn by each of the manufacturing costs. The ratio of manufacturing costs to sales shows the proportion of each pound's worth of sales that is spent on manufacturing the item. An efficient business expansion would cause this to fall as the firm obtained economies of scale, that is:

- reductions in unit production cost as a result of discounts on larger purchases of raw materials;
- full use of equipment on a greater volume of production;
- integration of processes;
- longer production runs to spread overheads over more units and so on as the business grows.

■ Machine efficiency

Machine efficiency before and after an expansion of scale and output can be measured by:

- the proportion of the working day that each machine is fully utilised;
- ratios of actual output to maximum possible output and of machine operating costs to the value of output;
- relationships between fixed and variable machine costs as the firm expands.

Ratios of pay to output, overtime to output, maintenance costs to output, machine set-up costs to output and the average costs of stoppages to output are also worthy of examination.

■ Labour efficiency

Work out the costs of supervising your employees (measured, perhaps, in terms of the amount of your own time that has to be devoted to this task) and divide this by the value of output before and after expansion. For what proportions of the working day are each of your employees fully occupied? What is the ratio of actual hours worked to 'productive' hours during which employees are directly contributing to the growth of the business? The ratio of total output to total hours worked is a telling figure, as is the simple ratio of labour cost to hours that employees are working. Labour cost can be divided by productive hours worked and then by actual hours worked. You might also look at the ratios of hours spent on maintenance, machine set-up, idle time and so on to total hours.

HOW TO AVOID UNPROFITABLE EXPANSION

There are two golden rules for business expansion:

- expand conservatively and circumspectly;
- never link management objectives to sales, but, rather, to unit profitability.

Conspicuous expansion might be avoided by increasing operations via a wholly owned subsidiary, discreet use of subcontractors (who are firmly instructed not to display the fact they are doing your work) or a joint venture with another firm. The latter course helps you spread the risk and financing requirements of an increased scale of operations, and it could enable you to acquire the experience and expertise of other people at very low cost. Alternatively, you might, perhaps, buy out another business – possibly a failing one that can be had for a negligible outlay – to carry your increased output under its own name, thus avoiding advertising the fact you are doing well and expanding operations. Current or potential competitors must not be alerted to your success or they might be encouraged to:

> *There are two golden rules for business expansion:*
>
> - *expand conservatively and circumspectly;*
> - *never link management objectives to sales, but, rather, to unit profitability.*

- extend their own operations;
- cut their prices;
- increase their advertising and sales promotions and so on;

thus sabotaging your capacity to grow. Driving around in an ostentatious motor car or otherwise openly pursuing an opulent lifestyle, might therefore, be damaging to your long-term future.

49

■ Look before you leap

Never accept a really large order without carefully considering all its implications for the welfare and development of the firm.

- Can you really cope with the extra work?
- Will you need to withdraw resources from other work or intended projects in order to complete the job and, if so, what are the likely consequences of this?
- What happens if the order is suddenly cancelled or if, having done the work, the customer is unable (or refuses) to pay?
- Are special designs, set-up costs or alterations in existing production methods necessary?
- How will you finance the acquisition of extra supplies and materials needed to produce the additional output?
- When will you be paid and what are the cash flow implications of various sets of credit terms?

If you do take the order, do not assume that it will be repeated or that it will lead to bigger and better things. Thus, always seek to expand output first by using existing resources more intensively. Run your machines for longer, stay open in the evenings and at weekends, have your current employees work overtime, subcontract and incorporate the extra costs incurred into a higher unit price, but do not expand the scale of your capital base until you are compelled to do so. Also, make absolutely sure that the sale of the higher output is assured. Note that rented machines, premises and equipment can be quickly and costlessly discarded, whereas assets purchased outright cannot be disposed of so easily.

Continuous monitoring of the consequences of changes in the scale of operations is essential. Predict the returns on every new asset you acquire and frequently compare actual and target returns. The targets quoted should relate to percentage rates of profit on each pound's worth of capital employed, not simply to the volume of sales. Expanding your operations may be the gateway to a fortune, but can so easily cause the failure of your firm.

If the problems outlined in this chapter sound familiar (and a few quick calculations should be sufficient to determine whether or not you are tending to overtrade), then you need to slim down your operations, rationalise and disinvest. These matters are considered further in later chapters.

SUMMARY

Rapid growth creates numerous difficulties, even for the highly profitable small business. Haphazard, disorganised and unplanned growth can even cause an expanding firm to collapse as its immediate financing needs outstretch its cash inflows in the short period.

It is essential that you understand how overtrading can occur and are able to recognise when it does in your own enterprise. This requires you to calculate a few key statistics in order to compare rates of return achieved before and after the firm's expansion. These statistics relate to your return on capital employed, the business' working capital and liquidity ratios, stock turnover rates and manufacturing indices.

When you expand, do so circumspectly. Never advertise the fact you are doing well or you could attract new competition. Inconspicuous growth may be achieved by the acquisition of another business, subcontracting or simply the more intensive use of existing labour and other resources. Never accept huge orders without first considering the implications of your firm becoming over-dependent on particular customers.

✓ Checklist

☐ Has the second of your employees worked as hard as the first? Did your third employee work as hard as the second?

☐ What is the relationship between the volume of your sales and the amount of credit you give to customers?

☐ Has the incidence of bad debt increased significantly within the last year, and, if so, why?

☐ Do you fully utilise every room in your premises?

☐ Are all your employees and equipment fully utilised throughout each working day?

☐ How much time do you spend working out employees' tax and National Insurance?

☐ Did you buy yourself a big car and otherwise visibly spend a lot of money on yourself when your firm began to grow?

☐ How did competitors react to your expansion?

☐ What is the average value of orders placed by customers?

☐ What proportion of your trade is conducted with customers who place low value orders? Is this trade financially worth while?

☐ Has the average period taken to deliver goods to customers increased since you started to grow?

☐ How sensitive is your firm's working capital to changes in its individual components?

☐ How can you improve your stock turnover ratio?

Cutting costs

1
2
3
4
5
6
7
8
9
10
11
12

INTRODUCTION

Two critical and obvious measures are necessary in any attempts to revive a business' fortunes – increasing the firm's revenues and reducing its costs. The former can occur as a result of:

- higher prices, made possible, perhaps, by repackaging the product, improving the image of the enterprise or entering the top end of a new market segment;
- increased turnover, created by aggressive selling, advertising and other sales promotions, possibly in conjunction with price cuts.

Policies for raising revenues need time to plan, research and implement. Cost reductions, conversely, are available now, and their cash flow benefits are felt immediately.

Low-profit businesses must be totally determined about cutting costs, concentrating on short-term expediency rather than the long-term consequences of reduced expenditure for efficiency and market share. Grasp the nettle. Aim to halve your administrative and secondary production costs. You may not achieve this, but the very process of trying will in itself be worth while.

Two things are needed for effective cost cutting – accurate information and an innovative and adventurous frame of mind. First, you must identify precisely the true cost structure of the firm. To do this you have to specify cost centres to which various expenditures may be ascribed.

COST CENTRES

Cost centres can be activities (packaging, advertising, assembly and so on), particular machines, products, offices or pieces of equipment, or individual members of your staff. If you choose a machine as a cost centre, then you work out all the costs of running that machine. Costs may also be assigned to a function, such as 'running the office'.

■ The need for a proper attitude

Effective cost reduction depends critically on your adopting appropriate mental attitudes towards running the business. It is useless, for example, to cancel your copy of the *Financial Times* while ignoring escalating costs of entertaining customers or servicing company vehicles. Be nihilistic – question every expenditure that arises, probe and analyse operations, and personally verify all invoices sent to the firm.

If you have employees, tell them about your deteriorating fortunes (they will find out anyway) and of the pressing need to reduce costs. It is essential that staff participate enthusiastically in reducing expenditures without your having to tell them what to do. They must want to switch off lights, save energy, economise on travel expenses and so on.

Target cuts should relate to specific cost centres rather than apply overall, as a general but vague commitment to reducing total costs is unlikely to succeed. Thus, the campaign needs careful planning, and detailed records of its subsequent success must be maintained. If a particular target reduction is not achieved, write out a detailed explanation of the reasons for failure. Look for cuts in each of the areas outlined below.

> *Effective cost reduction depends critically on your adopting appropriate mental attitudes towards running the business. It is useless, for example, to cancel your copy of the* Financial Times *while ignoring escalating costs of entertaining customers or servicing company vehicles.*

■ Administrative costs

Photocopying costs can be frightening, and excessive use of a photocopier must not be allowed. Unnecessary costs arise from taking too many copies – 20 when only 17 are needed, a round 100 instead of 83! Multiply these extras by the cost per copy and the frequency with which the practice of taking too many copies occurs and you have a substantial opportunity for reducing costs. To avoid this needless expense you could:

■ display a prominent notice on the photocopying machine reminding you and your staff only to take the actual number of copies needed;

- have all copying done by a person who is aware of the problem;
- place a restriction on the number of copies of a single document that anyone can take without permission.

Remember, too, that every photocopy taken and not thrown away creates the need for:

- extra space where it can be filed;
- someone to create and manage the file;
- the photocopied document to be physically filed away.

Any spare copies accidentally taken should be used as note paper.

Letters are expensive. Typing is the major cost, so, wherever possible, write notes on compliment slips to accompany enclosed documents rather than typing separate letters. Be sure you can justify every letter you despatch.

■ Avoid status differentials

It may not be a good idea for you to have better-quality furniture than your employees because this creates status hierarchies attached to having certain physical possessions – hat stands, filing aids, special chairs, desk accessories and so on – that cause petty resentments among the staff and cost money. If you have two employees, one of whom is paid more than the other, and if you personally have superior office furniture to the higher-paid employee, then you create a working environment in which they will want better accessories than the lower-paid member of staff. The more employees you have, the more you will then need to pander to their demands for status differentials.

It is better, I suggest, for you all to share the same office, have similar furniture (preferably secondhand, which is cheaper) and use the same equipment. By sharing an office, moreover, you are able to observe at first hand how hard your employees are working.

A common problem is for staff to jealously guard any item of furniture or equipment allocated to them, even after it ceases to be of practical use. Nothing is ever thrown away. Drawers, shelves and cupboards that should be used for stationery, component stocks and working equipment are used instead for storing personal belongings or become stuffed with out-of-date files. Turf out the lot. Start afresh with the absolute minimum of furniture, cabinets, filing units and similar equipment.

■ Offices

Offices have three functions:

- as places of work
- social environments
- they help represent the firm's 'corporate image' to the outside world.

Do you really need an office, though? Perhaps you can do your routine administration, filing, duplicating and so on at home.

You should certainly question whether or not the business needs its own photocopier. Why not negotiate a deal with the business next door whereby you use their photocopier (and perhaps other secretarial facilities) at just above marginal cost?

A good typist/secretary/administrator is a wonderful asset, but a bad one can cause havoc throughout your organisation. Secretaries need time off for holidays (perhaps at inconvenient times), occasionally fall ill, sometimes arrive late and leave early. You have to compute their tax and National Insurance and provide them with desks, typing chairs, potted plants and so on. Is it all really worth while? Couldn't you simply hire someone to come in one day a week (or even half a day) to do the accumulated typing? Again, why not pay for this from a neighbouring business? Another possibility is for you to dictate letters into a hand-held machine that you pass over once a week to a secretarial agency. There are few instances when business letters have to be typed and despatched in less than a week, and you can always use the phone or send a handwritten note in these circumstances.

DO-IT-YOURSELF ORGANISATION AND METHODS

Here's a short and simple programme for improving your administrative efficiency using the management consultant's technique of 'organisation and methods'. O & M is work study applied to clerical and administrative procedures, especially in relation to document creation, storage and retrieval. It aims to simplify work and avoid duplication of effort. Much clerical work involves paper, and the more unnecessary paperwork can be abolished the better. Thus, you should seek to eliminate redundant procedures, combine documents to reduce the number of documents produced and shorten the transit time for documents in circulation. Write out a list of all the clerical activities your business undertakes (issuing invoices, credit control, placing orders with suppliers and so on) and then ask the following questions in respect of each operation.

- *What is being done and how?*
- *What is the purpose of the activity? Is it connected with any other operation and, if so, how?*
- *Who performs the operation, and what special skills, training and experience are needed for its execution? Must a certain person (say, yourself) perform the operation or will anyone do?*
- *Where does the activity take place? Does it have to take place there and, if so, why?*
- *When are operations performed? Is starting one activity dependent on completing another? What will happen if the operation is not completed on schedule?*
- *How are operations completed. What equipment and other resources are necessary? Might alternative methods be used?*
- *What are the costs, including overheads, of individual operations?*

Answers to these questions often reveal cost-cutting possibilities. Also, the investigations needed to collect the required information should enable you to draft a 'flow chart' showing the movements of documents between various stages of processing. The best way to do this is for you to follow key documents (an invoice, for example) through your system. List everything that happens to the document. Each time you or an employee perform an operation on the document (such as filling in a form, calculating a figure, putting a letter into an envelope), draw a circle on the left-hand side of your description of the happening. Whenever you move a document between locations, draw an arrow on the left of that item on the list of events. Indicate a delay in processing the document (such as time spent, in an in-tray or out-tray) with a capital D. If you have to store the document in a filing cabinet or in a card index or similar device, show this with a triangle; if you inspect it (proofreading, checking for accuracy, reading the information it contains and so on), mark the item with a square. To illustrate, consider the progress of a supplier's invoice through your system. This might be recorded as follows.

Invoice received in post from supplier

1	○	Open letter
1	□	Read contents
1	→	Refer for checking against receipt of supplies
1	D	Hold in pending tray
2	□	Check that goods have been received as per invoice
2	○	Sign a 'goods received' slip
2	→	Send invoice to the accounts clerk
3	□	Hold in pending tray
3	□	Check amount owing against purchase order
3	○	Authorise payment
3	D	Clerk asks you for cheque
4	○	Record details from invoice in firm's ledger
1	→	File invoice
4	D	Cheque request held in pending tray
5	○	Write cheque
3	→	Return to accounts clerk
5	D	Holding in pending tray
6	○	Prepare accompanying letter/compliments slip for cheque
4	□	Check amount of cheque against invoice
7	○	Place cheque in envelope
6	D	Put envelope with today's mail and so on.

This is a simple example, but the approach can obviously be used for analysing more complicated events. Its advantage is that it forces you to investigate in detail every aspect of your clerical procedures, and such analyses frequently reveal many unnecessary delays and duplicated activities. The number alongside each symbol shows how often it has occurred at that point in the list. Look for high numbers, as they indicate excessively frequent operations, delays, document transits or inspections.

You may find that you can combine operations, complete two or three inspections in one go, or avoid delays by rerouting documents. The exercise should result in better coordination of activities, faster and simpler procedures, fewer clerical errors and tighter management control. Seek always to minimise the time spent shifting documents. Thus, workstations should be near to each other, and work should not be allowed to accumulate in one out-tray while the next in-tray in the system is empty.

■ Filing systems

You probably don't use more than a quarter of the information your internal administration generates. The widespread introduction of desktop computers has greatly increased the volume of data that a small business or SME can produce. All this information has to be stored (albeit electronically), and the extent of your filing operations can quickly assume terrifying dimensions.

Retain only the documents that are essential and discard the rest. Overly extensive filing systems waste space and create rigidities in organisations. The more you file, the longer it takes to locate essential documents, and the greater the probability of losing key facts.

File alphabetically under each of the firm's major activities. This is the cheapest of all filing methods because:

- no index is required;
- files can be referred to directly;
- the system is understandable, flexible and easy to use (although some cross-referencing might be necessary if your are unsure about which heading to apply to a particular document).

Never file documents relating to different functions in the date order they are received (with the possible exception of invoices) or dreadful chaos may ensue.

Cutting administrative costs is important, but do recognise the constraints involved. In most private companies, administration accounts for less than 10 per cent of total costs, so saving just a few photocopies (as opposed to continuous excessive use of photocopying facilities) will not contribute all that much to total profitability in the long run. It is perhaps better to identify the really big sources of expenditure (premises, raw materials, labour, processing, distribution) and seek economies there.

PREMISES

Bad choice of premises creates tremendous long-term problems for newly and recently established businesses. If your premises are clearly unsuitable for the purpose for which they were originally intended, you need to do something about it – and fast.

Perhaps you weren't sufficiently careful in your initial choice of building and/or location, and possibly you didn't look far enough ahead – premises suitable for the launch of a business might be totally inadequate for its subsequent operations. Have any of the following difficulties emerged?

- Inadequate parking space for customers or suppliers.
- Lack of custom due to insufficient numbers of your target consumer groups living around or commuting to the local area, and/or inadequate public transport facilities to support potential transient trade.
- Poor heating, gas, electricity and water supplies.
- Frequent break-ins.
- Too many competitors nearby.
- Difficulties in recruiting local staff who possess the skills needed by the firm.
- Remoteness of suppliers of raw materials, support services (waste disposal for instance) and so on.
- Intolerable noise outside.
- Exorbitant maintenance costs.
- Large areas of unused space in overly wide corridors, staircases and elsewhere.

If any of the above significantly reduce the efficiency of your business, you need to consider a move. However, first, ask yourself the simple, though incisive, question – 'Do I really need premises at all?'

■ *Working from home*

No time is spent travelling to work if you work from home. If you need to meet customers or suppliers only occasionally and your home is not a suitable venue, then perhaps you can hire a room in somebody else's premises for the odd half day. You cannot usually manufacture from home, but you can certainly run an office (see Note 1), while garages, attics and spare bedrooms can often be commandeered to provide storage space. Telephones, filing cabinets, photocopiers and office equipment do not work any less efficiently when located in a bedroom rather than on business premises. Also, you can hopefully use members of your family to do odd jobs for you for free (answering the telephone, filing or a little typing).

Your house contents insurance will not normally cover business equipment or stock, so check your policy and take out extra cover where necessary. Take care not to upset the neighbours. Delivery vans parked outside, callers who have the wrong address and go next door by mistake and so on will not help! If, for tax purposes, you claim that your home is a business say, by setting off domestic gas, electricity, and telephone bills against your profits – then your home ceases to be exempt from capital gains tax, which fact might make this course highly expensive in the long run.

■ **Low-cost premises**

If it is impossible to work from home, but you cannot afford to continue in your existing premises, then consider using a PO box number for your business mail and a professional answering service for incoming telephone

How much space do you really need? Space costs money – not only in terms of rent, but also for heating, lighting and business rates – so the less space you have, the lower the expense.

calls. The latter costs only a few pounds a week, and the personnel involved are adept at concealing the fact that callers are speaking to an agency rather than the receptionist of a business. You collect your calls daily and reply from home.

How much space do you really need? Space costs money – not only in terms of rent, but also for heating, lighting and business rates

– so the less space you have, the lower the expense. You might consider running the business from a single, tiny office in a low-rent part of town. Small offices are cheap to heat, light, ventilate and service. You don't need central heating (an electric fan heater will normally suffice) and rates are low.

■ Sale and leaseback

If you own your premises, consider subletting part of them or, if you are really short of cash, investigate the feasibility of a 'sale and leaseback' agreement.

Sale and leaseback means that you sell your land and building for just less than their current market value to a purchaser, who in return, contracts to lease the premises back to you for a certain period (five or ten years, perhaps) at a moderate rent. You will have to pay the legal fees involved in drafting the special contract, and you will probably be liable for capital gains tax on the disposal, but at least your firm survives.

■ Work space premises

'Work space' premises offer interesting opportunities to businesses that are hard up. These usually result from property developers or local authorities renovating old buildings and letting out floor space 'units' within them to small businesses or suites. You occupy part of the floor of a building (your 'share' of the floor may be delineated only by painted lines on the floor itself) and thus share heating, lighting and telephone switchboard facilities. In some schemes, you can also share the owner's secretarial, mailing and photocopying services (using your own headed notepaper and business documents, of course). There is a common cleaning service, and communal rooms for meetings and the reception of visitors. Business expansion can be accommodated by taking over adjacent work spaces. At the other extreme, it may be possible to rent 'touchdown' spaces for just a few hours a week, enabling you to collect messages and conduct urgent business.

There are problems involved in work space premises, though:

■ there is noise from neighbouring units;

- you lose privacy;
- your stocks, materials and equipment need special protection.

Also, units are typically let on a very short-term basis, subject, perhaps, to a single month's notice. Nevertheless, their low cost might be just what is needed for your business to survive.

Work space premises are not really suitable for firms that need impressive building fascias and interior decorations designed to project favourable images to outsiders. In this situation, you might select instead cheap alternative premises, but spend a lot of money on decorating the outside entrance and immediate reception area, with comfortable chairs, expensive low-level coffee tables, attractive lighting and colour schemes and so on. The rest of the building need not be so luxurious, save perhaps for a single small room used for interviewing visitors.

Keep the shabbiest parts of the premises well hidden from outsiders; people often connect dilapidated buildings with low-quality service from the firm, even though, in principle, this need not be the case.

PRODUCTION COSTS

Look carefully at the functions of your products. A product's 'function' in this context is a characteristic that makes it operate properly (such as by lifting a weight, heating a room, carrying goods, cutting a substance or whatever). You ask the question 'What is this product intended to do?' and then ask 'Is there a cheaper way of achieving this purpose?' In consequence, you may decide to abandon certain (costly to produce) designs, replace certain input materials with cheaper materials or change the process of manufacture. This approach is more suitable for products consisting of many component parts than for single-unit items as multicomponent products usually contain much scope for cost reduction in that unnecessary functions can be removed. Every single aspect of an item should possess an identifiable purpose, fulfilled at minimum cost and effort.

If you employ skilled labour, consider deskilling jobs to enable the work to be done by cheaper unskilled employees. Do skilled employees spend part of their time doing unskilled work? Can work be cheaply subcontracted to outsiders? Might overtime working be reduced or extra work be undertaken by part-time staff paid the standard rate?

Identify the sources of machine breakdown and implement measures to avoid these interruptions (by planned maintenance, for example). Look for ways to reuse scrap and waste materials (such as for packaging). Is the existing quality level of your input and output really necessary and how much could you save (bearing in mind the implications for marketing) by reducing quality?

Examine your purchasing policies critically. Would bulk purchasing at a discount outweigh the costs of storage and materials deterioration? Do you possess a proper search procedure for ascertaining the reliable sources of supply that cost the least?

■ Purchasing

It is too easy to continue using the same old suppliers and ignore cheaper and possibly better alternatives. Any potential supplier will be only too pleased to either send you literature or pay you a call. Have a policy of contacting at least one new supplying firm each month. You lose nothing other than a second class stamp for the letter asking for information, and perhaps half an hour of your time. Always ask suppliers to present estimates for exactly the same quantities and specifications, as then you are able to compare like with like when assessing quotations. Also, ask suppliers to include in their proposals a brief summary of:

- what they will do to ensure continuity of supply and prompt, regular deliveries (thus enabling you to economise on stockholdings);
- the extent of guarantees and after-sales service offered;
- you also need at least one reference from a business the firm has recently supplied.

■ Stockholding

Achieving lower stockholding by establishing a reliable delivery system is important for several reasons other than that it is wasteful tying up working capital (which represents an idle asset) in excessive stockholding. In particular:

- the more stock is held, the more is broken, naturally deteriorates or is pilfered;
- large stocks engender feelings of complacency among production staff, leading to sloppy work scheduling;
- storage, protection and security costs increase;
- the accumulation of stock necessitates installation of an expensive and complicated system for stock control.

■ Make or buy?

As there is no profit margin on components produced within the firm, and as you have complete control over their quality, design and time of delivery, you might conclude that it is always better to manufacture your own components than to buy them from outside, but this is not always the case. An external supplier will usually have produced many more units than those delivered to your firm and so will have obtained substantial economies from mass production (long manufacturing runs, use of specialist skilled labour and so on) and, thus, might well offer highly competitive prices as a result.

Consider also the fact that you might be able to delay payment for purchased component inputs, which means, in effect, that outside suppliers are lending you interest-free money. Moreover, you do not have to employ as much labour or use as much fixed plant or buy as much equipment (some of it having to be paid for now, in cash) as when you buy from outside.

MARKETING COSTS

Special problems apply here because certain aspects of marketing (especially advertising) generate income. A reduction in advertising is likely to reduce sales. Nevertheless, the effectiveness of current advertising should be regularly assessed and distribution and transport costs cut to the bone. Look for possible cost reductions in the following areas:

- packaging materials and equipment;

- costs of discounts and special offers;
- sales peoples' expenses.

■ Sales people

Sales staff paid hourly rather than on a commission basis can be extremely expensive to employ as a sales person who does not sell contributes little to the firm. Monitor the efficiency of your sales people and carefully analyse the number of calls they make, costs per call, costs per order, the order/call ratio and the average monthly profit contributed by each sales person. People sometimes forget the high costs of obtaining orders, so commission systems based on unit profitability per order (rather than on sales revenue or sales volume achieved) are usually more cost-effective.

Other marketing cost savings might be possible by:

- increasing a sales person's territory – and rewarding that person for their extra work;
- better route planning;
- analysing the returns on visits to various customer types.

Note the high cost of processing small orders. Costs of invoicing, credit control, packaging and despatch frequently make small orders unprofitable. Equally, the cost of providing after-sales service to small consumer units is alarming. Discounts given on small orders, transport costs, credit control expenses and the risk of bad debts may result in certain customers not being worth the effort involved.

Another costly activity is that of spending too much time selling to 'safe', established customers who are easy to do business with rather than seeking out completely new trade.

■ Mail order costs

Businesses that sell much of their output via mail order sometimes experience difficulty with actual or alleged non-delivery. Two costs are involved:

- the costs of the goods 'lost' in transit;
- the clerical and stationery costs associated with issuing payment

reminders, checking delivery details with the post office and so on.

Firms can insure against non-delivery with the post office, but the cost of cover may be substantial and there will be a delay before you are reimbursed. For small-value items, these hidden clerical costs can exceed the value of the goods and it might be better not to even bother trying to follow up small unpaid invoices relating to mail order delivery.

Normally, small-value mail orders should not be accepted unless they are clearly profitable or they are confidently expected to eventually lead to much bigger orders. Alternatively, you could impose a minimum price for small orders, regardless of their size. This fixed charge must be big enough to cover postage, packing, order processing, release from stores, invoicing and other clerical duties, and so on. Profit margins are thus maintained and unremunerative small orders actively discouraged.

■ Packaging and distribution costs

If you package your output in expensive containers, examine the feasibility of offering a sizeable refund on packaging materials returned to the firm. Possibly you can use the availability of the refund as a means of attracting repeat business, say, by inviting the customer to place a further order at a small discount available only at that time.

Weigh up the costs and benefits of distributing your products via a wholesaler rather than supplying retail outlets direct. By using a wholesaler, you lose control over its final resale price and your mark-up per unit of output is reduced (wholesalers buy in bulk and thus demand substantial discounts). However, several cost savings may accrue as by selling to a handful of wholesalers, you save:

- the expense of employing a sales person;
- travel costs involved in procuring small orders and other marketing expenses;
- warehousing and other stockholding costs (you are effectively using the wholesaler's warehouse to carry your stock);
- transport costs;

- the clerical work attached to issuing invoices to many retail outlets;
- credit control and debt recovery expenses, and the risk and costs of the inevitable bad debts.

On the other hand, using a wholesaler means you lose the ability to determine how your output is sold. There is no reason for a wholesaler to promote your goods rather than those of a competitor, and the wholesaler will recover all its stockholding and administrative costs by substantially raising your product's resale price, perhaps to a level which you feel detrimentally affects its sales prospects.

If you decide to supply retailers direct and if many outlets are involved, then note how much cheaper it is to deliver using your own vehicles rather than the vehicles of outside carriers or by rail, provided you have sufficient business to justify using a vehicle full time.

■ Transport

Vehicles are a major expense for most businesses. Compute the likely running and maintenance costs of any vehicle you wish to buy as well as its capital cost, and remember that its usefulness is more important than its comfort or prestige. Estate cars or MPVs are worth having because they can be employed as delivery vehicles as well as for transporting personnel. Make sure you absorb all the costs of transport into your product price and do not assume that the firm's car really exists for your own personal use.

INSURANCE

There are so many potential hazards associated with running a business that to insure against all of them may appear neither justified nor financially worth while. The high cost of insurance is one of the many unanticipated supplementary costs that new firms frequently ignore when drafting their first business plans. Thus, insurance

The high cost of insurance is one of the many unanticipated supplementary costs that new firms frequently ignore when drafting their first business plans. Thus, insurance bills often come as a shock and this may tempt some businesses to do without. However, to ignore insurance completely is to court disaster, so you need to think carefully about the risks, costs and benefits involved.

bills often come as a shock and this may tempt some businesses to do without. However, to ignore insurance completely is to court disaster, so you need to think carefully about the risks, costs and benefits involved.

■ Compulsory insurance

Employer's liability insurance is legally compulsory if you employ anyone full or part-time, on or off your premises. It covers your employees for any injuries that may take place during the course of their work.

Not legally compulsory, but virtually a must, for most businesses are:

- property (obviously), plant and equipment, stock and work in progress – any motor vehicles must, of course, be insured (commercial vehicles require separate insurance, while private vehicles used for business purposes need extra 'commercial use' policies);
- consequential loss – that is, compensation for loss of business and disruption following a disaster (quite apart from the loss of capital assets), ('key man' policies, which pay a lump sum on the death of the insured 'key' person, come under this heading);
- public liability insurance – to protect against liability to third parties killed or injured as a result of defects in the firm's premises or the negligence of employees.

You should also seriously consider insuring against:

- personal accidents;
- theft – including pilfering by staff, customers, break-ins and so on;
- goods in transit;
- 'professional liability' – that is, liability arising from wrongful and/or negligent professional advice given to clients;
- credit insurance – against defaulting customers;
- legal expenses insurance – to cover the legal costs of disputes in which the business innocently becomes involved;
- product liability cover – against defects in products causing injury to customers.

Together, these insurances add up to a considerable amount of money, and can substantially affect the business' cash flow.

Choosing which insurances to carry requires your having to manage risk. You must balance the substantial cost of cover against the possibly remote chance of loss. Do you really need all your insurances? Are you fully aware of the disclaimers and let-out clauses invariably hidden in the small print of your policies?

■ Managing risk

Risk is attached to most business operations. You can never be certain how much things will cost in the future, whether or not business conditions will change or what unexpected losses might occur (fires that destroy stock, for example). This does not mean you should insure everything – only that you must be fully aware of the extent of business risks. For instance, a market gardener knows there is a chance of night frosts in late spring that can wipe out crops. Yet, by planting later in the year, this risk (and the costs of insuring against it) can be avoided. The market gardener must therefore weigh up the benefits of planting early against the extra costs of insuring against abnormal weather.

■ Types of risk

You cannot insure against normal business risk. If, for example, the demand for your products suddenly falls, you alone must bear the consequences. Conversely, the risks of physical destruction of property and of natural disasters may be fully covered, as may 'social hazards', such as damage due to theft, forgery or civil riot.

Natural disasters cannot be prevented, but social hazards can sometimes be avoided. Thus, by carefully selecting your staff, checking references and not putting temptations for dishonesty before employees, you can minimise the risk of staff pilfering, possibly to the extent that insurance against this is not worth while. The more secure your premises, the fewer valuable goods you leave 'lying around', the more anti-shoplifting and other theft control devices you install, then the more you can economise on security insurance .

■ Other preventive measures

Other tips for reducing your business risk are to:

- fireproof buildings and materials;
- install sprinkler and alarm systems;
- make your employees safety and fire conscious;
- use a credit information service to avoid selling on credit to unsuitable customers;
- use security firms for high-value deliveries.

Never run water pipes (which can burst during cold weather) over valuable stores or equipment, and do not store goods in the basement if there is any chance of flooding. Use your common sense. If your premises are near a football ground or between two public houses in a rough area, then either have small windows instead of large, plate glass windows or invest in metal shutters. If your premises are in a district where there is a high risk of burglary, then install a good alarm system and make sure everything valuable is locked up or bolted down separately – make burglars work for their money! You should also ask for a visit from your local crime prevention officer, who can be contacted at the nearest police station.

■ Check your policies

If you choose not to insure against certain risks (such as window breakage, motor accidents other than third party), but, instead, create a reserve into which you pay a predetermined sum each quarter, then not only will you earn interest on your contingency deposits, but, also, you will know with certainty that you will be able to replace lost or damaged items. With insurance, on the other hand, you face another risk – that the insurance company (to which you have been contributing premiums for years) might not pay up (or may be extremely slow in paying) following a loss. Be particularly careful if you are running a business from home that your household policy is extended to cover your commercial activities.

■ Insurance principles and jargon explained

Insurers will only insure risks that are assessable, and even then they build into insurance contracts a number of devices to minimise the extent of their loss. You must have a personal interest in the thing insured. For instance, you cannot insure against other people's losses. Also, the principle of 'indemnity' always applies.

■ *Indemnity*

This means that you should only be placed in the same position after the loss that you were in before the loss occurred. On the face of it this seems fair enough – you ought not to be able to make a profit from insurance as then you would have an incentive to cause losses – by deliberately starting a fire, being careless, arranging for other people to steal your goods and so on. However, nasty shocks for insured people sometimes arise when the indemnity principle is applied.

Suppose, for instance, that your van is written off in a motor accident. The van is well maintained, regularly serviced and in excellent condition. In fact, it is almost like new and would cost several thousand pounds to replace. However, according to the insurance company, it only has a low 'book' value, and the insurer will only pay a few hundred pounds compensation for a vehicle of that year.

Similarly, you might insure your equipment for £20,000, lose a quarter of it in a natural disaster and claim £5000 compensation. 'Oh no!', says the insurance company after its loss inspection. The equipment, according to the insurance company, was initially worth £30,000, so in its opinion, you were 'underinsured' in the first place. Hence, it will only pay two-thirds of the £5000 (that is, £3333) on the basis that you had only insured two-thirds of the original total value of all your equipment.

Numerous problems also arise – determining the true value of specific replaceable items.

■ *Proximate cause*

This term means that insurance companies only accept liability if they believe a loss was caused 'proximately' (that is, immediately) by the occurrence of a risk specified in the insurance contract. Suppose, for instance, that all your windows are smashed by a gang of drunks. You claim for the loss you have incurred, but the claim is rejected because the insurer insists the damage was caused during a 'riot' or civil commotion and such events are not covered by the particular policy you hold! To take another example, suppose your stock is destroyed in a fire. An insurance company will want to know what caused the fire in the first place. If the ultimate cause was an event excluded from the contract (such as your negligence), you might not succeed in your claim.

■ Material facts

When taking out a policy you must not make a false statement, and must disclose all 'material facts' about your circumstances. A 'material fact' is any information that might influence the insurance company in deciding whether or not to insure you and, if so, at what rate of premium. If the information you provide is inaccurate or you simply forget about some matter that the insurer subsequently insists you should have disclosed, then the policy becomes void and the insurance company does not have to honour your claims.

Having decided which insurances you really need (cancel the others), go through each policy carefully, making quite sure you fully understand all the detail they contain. How much you are entitled to in the event of loss, and in what circumstances proper compensation might not be paid. Usually, insurance companies offer special policies that guarantee indemnity at replacement cost rather than second-hand market value. These policies – while more expensive – are certainly worth investigating.

FRAUD, THEFT AND CHEATING

Possibilities for fraud and theft exist within any business, especially those with many employees. There might be pilfering, shoplifting, goods sent to non-existent customers, cheques issued to non-existent suppliers, and so on. When employees undertake financial transactions on your behalf, it is normally better to have different people performing different tasks (sales records and cheques being issued by different people, for example) and, wherever possible, to mini-mise the practicability of collusion. Change the personnel undertak-ing these tasks regularly and without notice.

■ Cash and cheques

If your incoming mail regularly contains cash, postal orders or stamps, it is prudent to open the daily post yourself, though do this discreetly (say, by always being the first to arrive at work) so as not to appear dis-trustful of your employees. Bank your takings as often as possible – having lots of cash around invites theft. An advantage of trading under a business name rather than your own is that it becomes rather more difficult (though not impossible) for an employee to purloin cheques issued by your customers. If I trade as 'R. Bennett', then a dishonest employee might open a bank account falsely using my name and pay into that account some cheques addressed to me. The employee might then forge and/or falsify internal documents to avoid discovery of the theft, at least in the short term. If, conversely, I trade as 'RHA Man-agement Consultancy' and ensure that customers write cheques in favour of that name, then the dishonest employee must convince a bank that a legitimate business exists under that name prior to open-ing the account. This is not impossible, but the trouble involved may discourage an opportunist thief.

■ What theft is

Problems arise over the definition of theft, especially where employees have free access to materials and equipment and are encouraged to take work home in the evenings. Theft means dis-honest appropriation of someone else's property with the intention of permanently depriving the other person of that property. It is not dishonest to take property if the person genuinely believes that it belongs to them, or believes sincerely that its owner has consented or would consent to the property's removal. Be absolutely clear, therefore, about what equipment may or may not be removed from the building by your staff.

MANAGING YOUR TIME

The biggest of your administrative expenses could, in fact, be the cost of your own time. Think of time as a resource, a raw material, and seek to allocate your time in the most productive ways. Time spent writing an unimportant letter, for example, might be better used visiting a customer or inspecting the quality of supplies, so rank your activities in order of importance and consciously adjust the time you spend on each job.

The biggest of your administrative expenses could, in fact, be the cost of your own time. Think of time as a resource, a raw material, and seek to allocate your time in the most productive ways.

■ Avoid interruptions

The efficient use of time requires your maximising the creative output of each working day. This is not as easy as it may first appear. The sorts of activitities a small business or SME owner undertakes (meeting people, talking on the phone, writing letters, dealing with customers and suppliers, inspection, day-to-day decision making, forward planning and control and so on) are varied, scattered and prone to frequent interruption.

■ Sources of interruptions

Many interruptions arise from routine communications that disrupt more creative work. Set aside some predetermined part of your day (between 2 and 3 o'clock in the afternoon, for example, by which time all the day's mail will have been delivered) and handle communications during that period. Stick to this rigidly – if outgoing letters cannot be completed within the time allotted to communication duties, then leave them until the following day when they will be given priority. Also, wherever possible:

- deal with each item of correspondence only once – it is surprising how often the attention paid to certain letters is duplicated;
- group together similar tasks – write all your letters in one go, make your phone calls one after another and, when you use the phone, have before you all necessary information and a list of the points you wish to make;

- write notes on the outcome of a call immediately after it finishes
  – if you see outside people, try to see them by appointment and
  during a prearranged period of time.

■ Plan your working day

Great anxiety, overexertion and stress can result from trying to keep
abreast of current communications duties while simultaneously pursuing more creative goals. Hence, you should:

- forecast your future workload, assign priorities and plan your time;
- predict how much time you need for particular jobs, record the
  times actually taken and analyse any differences.

To avoid the accumulation of a large backlog of petty administration, reserve a limited time slot each week in which to do routine
work alone. The best time for this is when you are tired as doing
mundane, non-critical duties is a source of relief from the exhausting effects of more demanding activities and so can be relaxing.

Undertake critical tasks when you are fresh and most creative. If
you normally feel energetic in the early morning, do your difficult
work then. If, conversely, you 'warm up' during the day, then do
mundane work in the mornings and leave creative activities until
later in the day.

People commonly do the reverse of all this, using their intellectu-
ally productive hours for work that is interesting but does not require
them to exercise discretion or intense mental effort. Suppose, for
example, you are most alert in the mornings. You open your mail at
9.00 am and immediately become interested in petty administrative
matters, which occupy you for three or four hours. When, eventually, you come to consider more substantial issues, you are too tired
to attend to them properly, so they are put aside and never fully
resolved! Use the above pointers to maximise your effectiveness.

SUMMARY

**Effective cost-cutting requires that you assume an appropriate atti-
tude of mind as well as investigating the costs of particular business**

activities. Profligate firms rarely survive in the longer term, so the adoption of a proper perspective on costs and revenues is essential for the future well-being of the enterprise.

Crucial to the success of any cost-cutting exercise are:

- the definition of relevant cost centres
- the accurate measurement of costs, although for firms which produce many products there is no easy way of apportioning overheads to cost centres – all systems for allocating indirect costs are necessarily subjective to some extent.

Question the need for every significant item of expenditure and, in the short term, use zero-base budgeting. Seek economies in production, the utilisation of premises, distribution and general administration. Recognise, however, that administration typically accounts for only a small part of total expenditure and, hence, to achieve really big savings you will probably have to look elsewhere.

Simplify your ordering and stockkeeping system, and reduce to the absolute minimum the average amount of stock you hold. Be fully aware of the risk of your stores being pilfered (and of other forms of theft and cheating) and implement appropriate measures to pre-empt such difficulties.

Efficient management of time is critically important for the owner of a small business or SME. Time is a resource, to be allocated as rationally as raw materials or any other input to the firm. Plan your time, avoid interruptions at inconvenient moments and try to complete your work in blocks consisting of tasks of a similar nature.

✓ Checklist

☐ What is the proportion of administrative cost to the total cost of running your business?

☐ How recently did you undertake a thorough analysis of the costs attached to a particular aspect of the firm?

☐ Have you prepared budgets for next month, next quarter and the next half year? If not, why not?

☐ How much have you spent on the furniture and equipment used by yourself compared to that of each of your employees?

☐ List six reasons for needing an office for your business.

☐ Go through the filing cabinet nearest to your desk and calculate the proportions of essential to non-essential information that it contains.

☐ Are your premises fulfilling the purposes for which they were originally intended? If not, why not?

☐ Find three alternative locations for your business and establish what the rent and rates payable on suitable premises in those areas are.

☐ Have you investigated whether or not the functions your output serves might be equally well served by a product that costs less to produce?

☐ What could you have done to avoid your last three equipment break-downs?

☐ Find the names and addresses of three alternative suppliers of your primary raw material.

☐ How much would it cost to arrange for the input components you presently buy from outside to be manufactured or assembled within your own business?

☐ Is a large proportion of your total sales accounted for by a small number of customers?

☐ What measures have you introduced to avoid your stores being pilfered?

☐ How much time did you spend making unproductive telephone calls last week?

Note

1. You do need planning permission from your local authority. This is normally given without question, provided your business will not cause a nuisance to neighbours. If your property is leasehold and/or carries a mortgage, you must check these to ensure that the lease or mortgage agreement does not prohibit the use of the property for business purposes. Note that there exists a 'grey area' between domestic and commercial activities and you do need to exercise discretion. Building societies are usually prepared to adjust the terms of a mortgage to allow business use of domestic property in appropriate circumstances.

How to collect a debt

Introduction • The cost of credit • Credit checks
Improve your credit control • Debt collecting
How to take somebody to court • Enforcement
Problems of legal action • Summary • Checklist

INTRODUCTION

Not all firms find it necessary to give credit – wine bars, restaurants, small shops and certain other retail outlets are examples of businesses that typically trade in cash. Yet, the majority of businesses cannot survive unless they offer their customers reasonable periods in which to settle bills. Two questions immediately arise – how long is a 'reasonable' period and what do you do when a customer is obviously not willing to settle an outstanding account.

THE COST OF CREDIT

Credit is outrageously expensive as you lose money every time a customer delays payment of a bill. If a £1000 invoice falls due on 1 January and is not paid until 31 March, you lose the use of £1000 for a quarter of a year. At worst, you could have put this £1000 into an account at The Post Office, for example, and earned three months' interest. More profitably, you could have employed the money collected on 1 January to buy further inputs (labour, raw materials, stock and so on), have processed them and sold the resulting output in order to achieve even greater returns.

By letting customers extend payments in this way, the intensity of your 'trading cycle' is severely reduced – you 'turn over' your sales revenue less often than you should. Looking at the problem from another perspective, just suppose your customers take an average of six weeks to settle their bills and that you sell an average of £2000-worth of goods each week. You have already paid for the labour, raw materials and overheads used in each week's £2000-worth of sales, so, at any moment in time, you need six weeks times £2000, – that is, £12,000 of finance – straight from your own pocket, simply to run the firm! Reduce the credit period to three weeks and you instantly release £6000-worth of working capital. If a debt becomes 'bad' (that is, the customer never pays), this can cost your business a great deal of money, particularly if you are trading on low profit margins. Chasing debts can also cost you in terms of time. Obviously, you need to be as diligent as possible in chasing debts!

CREDIT CHECKS

Although the need to offer credit must be accepted as an inevitable fact of business life in most circumstances, always recognise the adverse effects that slow settlement of debtors' accounts will exert on your firm's operations, and that the decision as to whether or not to give credit is yours alone. Certain customers may go bankrupt, owing you large amounts of money, and there exists the possibility of deliberate credit fraud by some clients. This latter risk can be minimised by carefully checking out the creditworthiness of customers who demand credit facilities. Ask the customer to complete a form requesting a credit account and for a banker's reference. The form should ask for the following information.

> *Although the need to offer credit must be accepted as an inevitable fact of business life in most circumstances, always recognise the adverse effects that slow settlement of debtors' accounts will exert on your firm's operations, and that the decision as to whether or not to give credit is yours alone.*

- Name and address of the customer's bank and when an account with that bank was first opened. You need to be suspicious if the business claims to be well established, yet the account was only opened within the last couple of years, bearing in mind how easy it is to open a new account using a false name and address. If the account is, say, less than two years old then ask for details of the customer's previous bank and for permission to approach the previous banker for a reference.
- The customer's home address if this differs from their business premises.
- If the customer is a limited company, its registration number and date of incorporation.
- Names and addresses of any partners in the customer's business.
- The name and address of at least one other firm presently supplying that customer on credit, plus permission to approach that firm for a credit reference.

■ Credit control agencies

A credit control agency will prepare and issue such a form on your behalf on payment of a small fee and will, moreover, inspect centralised County court records to check whether or not the customer is in the process of being declared bankrupt or, if it is a company, wound up or has any County court judgements awaiting settlement or any outstanding court enforcement orders or attachment of earnings orders (see below). If the customer is a limited company, the agency will inspect its documents at Companies House (although you can do this yourself either by post or by visiting Companies House) to see the extent of its mortgages and charges (see Chapter 11) and will report back to you on its findings.

■ Credit limits

Acting on the information you have gathered, you can now set credit limits (a good figure would be the expected value of three months' sales to each company in question).

■ Credit refusal

You may prefer to refuse credit altogether. This means either not trading with the company at all or insisting on cash before or on delivery. Cash before delivery can be achieved by pro forma invoicing the customer and perhaps arranging for an agreed percentage of the value of the pro forma invoice to be paid up front.

■ Need for security

For very large credit transactions, you will want a binding assurance that you will eventually get your money, regardless of the state of the customer's trade. Effectively, you are lending to the customer during the credit period and it is only reasonable that the loan be secured, as if it were a loan from a bank. Security might be offered to you in the form of a fixed charge on the firm's assets or your retaining title to the goods until payment occurs. If the customer is a limited company, you will need at least one of its directors to offer a personal guarantee – enforceable on their personal estate – that the debt will be honoured. These options require legal advice, the cost of which should be incorporated into the price of the output.

■ Reservation of title

When you sell on credit, you accept that the purchaser can sell the goods to a third party prior to your being paid. If your credit customer then reneges on the debt, you must try to collect the money from that person or firm; you cannot normally approach the third party and reclaim the goods that in law, now belong to the third party. The exception is where the firm builds into its terms of sale a 'reservation of title' clause whereby you retain legal ownership of the goods until you have been paid.

This is not a straightforward matter as the circumstances in which courts will accept the legitimacy of such contracts are complicated and so you must consult a solicitor before attempting such a sale. However, the possibility is perhaps worth investigating if your output was a high value and is such that its reclamation from customers in a resaleable condition is practicable.

■ How title to goods may be 'reserved'

A reservation of title (RT) clause makes the transmission of ownership of property conditional on receipt of payment. There are two types of RT clause – 'simple' and 'extended'. The former occurs in the circumstances already outlined – that is, where the seller retains ownership until cash payment is received or a cheque is cleared. This is legal under both the UK Sale and Supply of Goods Act 1994 and European Union law. More difficult, however, are 'extended' RT clauses, which take one of the following two forms.

- The buyer is regarded as an agent of the supplier and, if the goods are sold to a third party, the money received is viewed as being 'held in trust' on the supplier's behalf. Thus, should the first buyer become insolvent before paying the supplier, the latter has a charge (see below) on that firm's assets, even to the point of being able to reclaim the goods in question from the third (or subsequent) parties to whom they were resold.

- The clause may state that if the goods supplied are used as inputs (that is, as raw materials) to other goods, then the original supplier retains a financial interest in the final goods that result, unless the final goods possess a different 'commercial identity' from the original goods input. For example, a case in 1983 (see Note 1 at the end of this chapter) established that a supplier of leather to a handbag manufacturer did not have title to handbags sold to the public by the manufacturer, despite the existence of an extended RT clause.

IMPROVE YOUR CREDIT CONTROL

First, you must calculate how long, on average, it takes to collect a debt. An indication of this period can be obtained by using the following formula:

$$\frac{\text{Amount owed to you at the end of the year}}{\text{Total value of sales during the year}} \times 52$$

Thus, if your business sold £100,000 of goods last year, but was still owed £25,000 at the year's end, the average credit period suggested by the formula is:

$$\frac{15,000}{100,000} \times 52 = 13 \text{ weeks}$$

Of course, an exceptionally big order already delivered but not yet paid for immediately prior to the end of the financial year could distort this figure by misleadingly increasing the value of debtors on the top of the formula. So, take a random sample of, say, 50 invoices issued during the last year (and I assume here that invoices are properly issued the moment goods are despatched) just to check that the average debt collection period revealed by the formula does actually represent the true situation.

■ Identify overdue accounts

Next, devise a system (a simple system will suffice, and there are several commercial systems on the market) for identifying overdue accounts the instant they are in arrears. The system must enable you to gather together all invoices that are, for example, one week overdue, two weeks overdue, one month overdue, two months and so on. Dated cardboard folders might be all that is required to generate this information in the required form, but whichever way you do it, you will probably find that a handful of customers predominate in the records for long overdue accounts and you need to seriously consider whether or not continuing to service these customers is financially worth while (the profit mark-up on transactions with such customers might be effectively wiped out by the implicit costs of delays in payment).

■ Know your customer

On the other hand, late payers may be big and valued customers who can be relied upon to pay eventually. In this case, you should time your invoices to coincide with customers' accounting systems, details of which you can obtain by phone. There is no reason for customers to be unwilling to tell you the day of the month they settle invoices and, importantly, the names and telephone extensions of the staff involved. Once you have established a personal relationship with the accounts clerk (sometimes called ledger clerk) who deals with your bills, you can telephone them to ensure that high-value invoices are internally processed (checking for numerical accuracy, inspecting the goods and so on) on time. The purchasing and accounts departments of large organisations can be extremely helpful in these respects.

DEBT COLLECTING

Much time, effort and money is taken up in writing letters, making telephone calls, issuing copy invoices and so on in order to collect overdue accounts. It might be worth while, therefore, considering offering customers an inducement to settle early by, say, offering a discount for prompt payment. Unfortunately, however, such discounts are extremely expensive – a 2.5 per cent discount offered for payment within 30 days actually works out at a staggering 30.4 per cent on an annual basis (remember you are giving the discount 365/30 times per year, which, multiplied by 2.5, gives an annual percentage rate of 30.4).

You could instead consider giving discounts for very large cash orders. Money lost on discounting is recovered by means of increased sales volume. The threshold for discount can be tailored to appeal to new customers in new market segments. Better, perhaps, and more important, is a rigorous system for politely pursuing debtors the moment their accounts are overdue.

Prepare two standard letters asking for settlement of unpaid bills. One should be sent two weeks after the account is due, the other two weeks later. If you are not very good at writing letters, go to your local library and borrow a book of standard business letters, any one of which will contain examples of letters for credit control.

■ Don't be afraid to use the telephone

If the account is still unsettled, use the telephone. Take care in how you make this call as much hinges on the customer's response, especially if your business is desperately short of funds. A direct and poignant appeal for prompt settlement (even if the bill is not all that much overdue) can evoke a sympathetic and potentially life-saving response. When making the call:

> *A direct and poignant appeal for prompt settlement (even if the bill is not all that much overdue) can evoke a sympathetic and potentially life-saving response.*

- jot down the major details of the invoice and the points you wish to make, and be sure you speak to someone in a position to expedite payment, preferably the relevant accounts clerk;
- explain the position briefly and check that the listener understands what you have said;
- be brief, and always polite – nothing guarantees that a slow-paying, but honest, customer will impose further delays more than offending a sensitive accounts clerk.

Ring in the morning so that if details have to be checked at the other end, your contact can telephone you back later in the day. If your contact does not return the call, you then have an excuse to ring again. Do not fear being nervous when making such a call – indeed, obvious nervousness in your voice might actually help your case in that it emphasises to the listener the urgency of the matter in relation to your cash flow.

■ The next step

If the call does not result in payment, wait another week or so and call again. Thereafter, there is little point making further telephone calls – more formal and severe measures are now required. However, before initiating tough debt-collecting action, first ask yourself why the customer refuses to pay the bill. They might simply be hard up and, if so, there is little point in your spending much time chasing the debt. If the customer is also in business, try to think of a way the bill might be settled in kind, say by the firm doing some work for you free or extract an agreement (which needs to be in writing) that the customer will supply you with some of its output at cost price (so that you can sell the goods at a profit) as soon as its trading position strengthens. A debt collection agency (see below) will not purchase a debt from you if the possibility of settling the bill is remote, and there is no point in going to court if the debtor obviously hasn't the means to pay a substantial part of the amount owing.

Your best strategy here is to minimise your loss. If, instead of cash, the creditor offers physical goods that have a resale value, you should take them – you have nothing to lose.

If, conversely, the debtor is clearly solvent, yet still refuses to pay you have three options:

- trying to collect the debt yourself by making a personal visit;
- selling the debt to an agency;
- recovering the debt through the courts.

The first option – personal attempt to recover the debt – is perhaps the least attractive. Debt collecting in Britain is covered by section 40 of the Administration of Justice Act 1970, plus the precedents established by a number of test cases brought under this Act and others (see Note 2 at the end of the chapter). Of course, it is illegal to use or threaten violence or even to harass unduly those who owe you money. Courts have ruled that, for example, calling on someone's home late at night is unlawful (as is sending several men or a man with a large dog!). Other unlawful practices include:

- approaching a member of a debtor's family and making abusive or threatening suggestions;
- pretending to be a policeman or court official or threatening criminal (rather than civil) proceedings;
- discussing a person's debts with their neighbours or posting notices about the debt in shop windows near to where the customer lives.

You have to play strictly by the book, though, by all means, visit the debtor to establish the cause of non-payment. Perhaps they have been ill, face temporary cash flow problems or have simply behaved irresponsibly in some way.

■ Using an agency

The second alternative is to use an agency for collecting the debt (agencies can be found in *Yellow Pages*). Either you can pay an agency a hefty commission on the value of the final settlement or you can sell the debt outright in exchange for cash. This enables you to convert the debt into some cash (provided the agency believes it will be able to recover the amount owing), but it is very expensive as you only get a percentage of the amount due – perhaps as little as 25 or 30 per cent.

An interesting and potentially useful variation on the collection agency theme is the use of an agency letterhead, even if you do not feel that extensive further action to recover the debt (including court action) is financially worth while, especially if the amount is too low to interest a collection agency *per se*. In return for a small fee, some agencies will send an impressive letter to the recalcitrant debtor saying the agency has been instructed by you to initiate legal proceedings to recover the amount owed. This might shock the debtor into payment as slow payers are often more impressed by correspondence from a seemingly bona fide debt collector, which the debtor assumes will take legal action, than from a small firm the debtor assumes does not possess the knowledge or resources necessary to pursue the debt. In fact, of course, you have no intention of taking the customer to court and are using this device merely as a ruse to engender settlement. Some businesses even invent non-existent agencies with nothing more than a mailing address behind them just for this purpose.

> *Slow payment of outstanding balances can cause acute embarrassment regarding your own consequent inability to settle debts, and honouring them in the absence of a cash inflow may result in your accumulating a substantial overdraft. Do not conceal from the bank the fact that you are experiencing problems in collecting debts. Banks, after all, are themselves intimately involved in the debt business and so bank managers typically possess great experience in this field*

■ Tell your bank

Slow payment of outstanding balances can cause acute embarrassment regarding your own consequent inability to settle debts, and honouring them in the absence of a cash inflow may result in your accumulating a substantial overdraft. Do not conceal from the bank the fact that you are experiencing problems in collecting debts. Banks, after all, are themselves intimately involved in the debt business and so bank managers typically possess great experience in this field. Your bank may be able to put you in touch with a respectable debt collector or 'credit factor' who will purchase (at a discount) for cash the invoices you issue to customers and will then collect for themselves the amounts owed.

HOW TO TAKE SOMEBODY TO COURT

Ultimately, you will have to take an unrepentant debtor to court. You should realise, however, that this is not cheap and is likely to be time-consuming.

If the debt is less than £1000, then, unless the case involves complicated matters of law or if fraud is alleged, you must use the County court 'small claims' procedure. This – in comparison with standard County court proceedings – reduces the formality and inconvenience involved, although all court appearances are harrowing to some degree. Cases involving amounts of more than £1000 can be settled using the small claims procedures, provided both parties agree to this. There is no jury – cases are adjudicated by either a judge or, if the amount claimed is relatively low, by a 'registrar' sitting alone. Proceedings in small claims cases are intended to be conducted in a straightforward manner and so you are not obliged to use a solicitor. If you do choose to be represented when using the small claims procedure, you cannot claim your representative's costs from the other side if you win the case (although minor administrative costs are recoverable, see below).

■ Starting an action

You begin the action by obtaining from your local County court (the address and telephone number will be in your telephone directory) a 'particulars of claim' form, which you complete (only brief details of the case are required) and return. Alternatively you can type out your own 'particulars of claim' on a separate sheet of paper under this heading. You state the facts of your claim and the sum of money you are owed. If you wish, you can visit the County court office in person and do this 'over the counter' then and there.

■ The summons

The cost of initiating an action is very low. You next complete a 'request' form, from which the court prepares a 'summons', which is served on the debtor. The request is a simple document, and the court staff will help you complete it 'over the counter' if you so desire. The court now sends the 'defendant' (that is, the person or firm that owes you money) the summons containing details of the allegation and gives the defendant 14 days in which to reply. If the summons is returned undelivered, the court will tell you about this and you will then normally ask the court bailiff to serve the summons on the defendant in person. An additional (recoverable) fee is payable for this work. You receive a 'plaint note', which formally registers the case, allocates a number to the case, and is accompanied by a notice giving a date for the hearing. Four possibilities now arise.

- The debtor pays up, in which case you are entitled to claim from the defendant the fee you had to pay for initiating the case.
- No payment is received and the defendant does not reply to the summons that has been served on them either by post or by the court bailiff. The court now sends you a form called a 'request for entry in default', which is a statement of when you want the money (including the cost of issuing the summons) to be paid. The form is easily completed and no technical legal jargon is involved.
- The debtor admits the claim and asks for time in which to pay the amount owed. In this case, the debtor must complete a form listing their means and assets and set out any offer they wish to make. If you refuse an offer of partial lump sum settlement, the court will fix a date for the court registrar to decide how the debt is to be paid (perhaps in instalments).
- The case is contested (that is, the defendant replies to your summons and appears in court). Should the debtor reply to the summons and state that they will contest the case, but then fails to turn up for the hearing, you will normally win the case automatically, and be able to claim from the defendant your travelling expenses to attend the hearing and small expenses for witnesses. Otherwise, the case is heard in the usual way.

■ Arbitration

As mentioned, cases involving more than £1000 can be settled in a manner similar to the small claims procedure, provided both parties agree. The advantages of this (referred to as 'arbitration') compared to a formal trial are that:

- the hearing is held in private, not in open court;
- procedures are relatively informal – the strict rules of evidence do not apply;
- the arbitrator – normally the court registrar, although any suitable person may be appointed if both parties so desire, can adopt any procedures that may consider fair, convenient and appropriate for expediting the case.

However, solicitors' costs will be allowed in disputes concerning more than £1000 unless both parties agree to their exclusion.

The side that loses an arbitrated case does not have the same rights of appeal as the loser of a dispute tried in the conventional manner. Appeals from arbitrated judgements are complicated, costly and need to rely on some proven incompetence or inconsistency on the part of the arbitrator.

If you win any kind of County court case and the defendant does not pay up, it is your responsibility to 'enforce' the judgement.

ENFORCEMENT

Unfortunately, winning a case is not the end of the story. You may now have to enforce settlement of the debt, as responsibility for making the debtor pay up after a court order has been issued lies with you, not the court. Enforcement can be tedious and expensive, so think carefully before embarking along this road. There is absolutely no point in proceeding if the debtor has no money or assets to sell (bankruptcy of the debtor might be a better option in this case as, when bankruptcy proceedings are threatened, previously undisclosed assets sometimes suddenly appear), but, enforcement costs are recoverable from the debtor if you do eventually succeed.

■ Enforcement proceedings

The judgement order issued by the court following your successful action will require the debtor to pay the money owed either at once or in instalments. You begin enforcement proceedings immediately an outstanding amount becomes overdue. If you know the debtor has assets, move straight away to one of the enforcement methods outlined below. Otherwise, a further court hearing may be required to establish the extent of the debtor's assets.

To arrange this, you write to the County court covering the area in which the debtor resides, asking for an 'oral examination' of that person (or of the company secretary or named director of a limited company, although, in this case, you are only allowed to ask about the company's assets and not the private means of its directors). The court sends you a form that you complete and return with the appropriate fee. This fee is increased periodically, but does not amount to more than a few pounds. Then the court arranges a date and venue for the examination and issues an order to the debtor to attend. Failure to obey this order can result in a prison sentence for contempt of court.

At the hearing, you ask (or get the registrar in charge of the hearing to ask) for particulars of the debtor's income from employment (if any) and from other sources, the income of the debtor's spouse, details of bank and building society accounts, ownership of stocks and shares, property and so on, and whether or not that person is owed any money and, if so, by whom. There are five ways of enforcing settlement, outlined below. Which option you choose depends on the specific circumstances surrounding the case.

■ *Attachment of earnings*

If the debtor is working for someone, the best solution may be to ask the court to order the debtor's employer to pay part of the debtor's weekly or monthly earnings direct to you. The amount payable is decided by the court, taking into account the debtor's need to support their family.

You apply for this type of order on a form, in which you specify the debtor's employer and place of work. A small fee is payable when you return the form. The court then serves the application on the debtor by post. If there is no reply, you will have to pay the court bailiff to serve the application personally. No further action is possible until the application is served, so if the debtor has moved, you need to discover their new address before proceeding further.

■ *Attachment of debts*

The debtor might be owed money by someone else (referred to as a 'garnishee') who can be ordered by the court to pay the amount owed (or some part of it) to you instead of the debtor. This is useful where the debtor is unemployed but known to have money in a bank or building society account as money in such an account is technically 'owed' to the customer. The problem, of course, is that as soon as debtors get wind of the fact that 'garnishee orders' are being sought against them, they immediately withdraw all the money from their bank and other accounts. Moreover, a garnishee order applies only to the money held in an account on the day the order is served on the bank, not to money paid in thereafter.

To obtain a garnishee order, you must go in person to your local County court, complete a form, swear on oath before a court official that the information given is true and pay the relevant (subsequently recoverable) fee. The order is served on the bank or other debtor of the debtor who owes you money. On receipt of a garnishee order, the third party pays the amount due into court (assuming enough money is available in the account) after deducting a small fee for its clerical expenses.

■ *Warrant of execution*

This is the commonest of the methods. It means that the court directs a bailiff to seize and sell sufficient of the debtor's assets to settle the outstanding balance. The warrant instructs the bailiff to visit the debtor's house, business premises or anywhere else the debtor's goods might be found and physically remove and sell whichever goods the bailiff thinks will raise enough money to cover the debt, plus the cost of removing them and putting them up for auction. Clothing and bedding up to a certain value cannot be taken, nor can the debtor's 'tools of trade'.

Although warrants of execution are frequently used, problems do occur, specifically:

- the bailiff cannot force entry to the debtor's home – although business premises can be so entered, and refusing to allow the bailiff to enter domestic premises will eventually result in the debtor going to jail;
- costs of removing, storing and selling goods can exceed their auction value, and if the bailiff believes the amount raised will not cover these costs, then the goods will not be taken;
- some, if not all, of a debtor's valuable household goods (refrigerators, television sets and so on) may have been obtained on unexpired hire purchase and cannot be seized as they do not 'belong' to the debtor;

- only goods belonging to the debtor can be taken, not those belonging to the debtor's spouse or any other person.

To obtain a warrant, you complete a form and pay a small fee that varies according to the value of the outstanding debt. You must find and give to the bailiff the debtor's current address. If you know the whereabouts of any of the debtor's property, you should tell the bailiff.

Equitable execution

This is appropriate where the debtor receives rent or other regular, non-employment payments and/or proceeds from the sale of land. The court will appoint a receiver who collects these payments and turns over the money to you. Heavy administrative costs are involved, and you need proper legal advice before attempting this procedure.

Charging orders

A charging order is an order preventing the debtor selling their land or securities (stocks, shares and debentures) until the outstanding debt has been settled. The debtor must own the land or securities before the charge is imposed.

This method is useful where the debtor's major asset is a house or portfolio of shares and they have little money income. Charging orders can be extended to force the debtor to sell the land or securities in order to settle the outstanding balance, but special court proceedings are necessary before this may occur, and the process is complicated and expensive.

Declaring a debtor bankrupt

If none of these measures succeeds in obtaining the money, you can apply to have the debtor declared bankrupt as non-compliance with a judgement or order is one of several acts that render the debtor liable to bankruptcy (or company liquidation) proceedings. The threat of bankruptcy, plus all that it involves (see Chapter 12) might prompt a debtor who – via various delaying tactics, changes of address, withdrawal of funds from bank accounts, putting goods in other peoples' names and so on – has messed you around for months to suddenly settle the debt (and previously accumulated collection expenses).

PROBLEMS OF LEGAL ACTION

Clearly, there are many problems and pitfalls associated with legal action and you should never rush into litigation if you have any doubts about the strength of your case. Note, moreover, that there is nothing to prevent the debtor using a solicitor in a small claims action, hence injecting formality and legal jargon into the proceedings and leading, perhaps, to your having to hire a solicitor yourself and solicitors' fees are not recoverable if the debt is under £1000.

Delaying tactics by the defendant – making vague promises, changing address, opening and closing bank accounts, offering trivial defences to the claims you present, asking for adjournments, shuffling assets – can wear you down to the point where you simply haven't the energy to proceed. Also, you might feel fundamentally ill at ease in a court environment. Court registrars are themselves lawyers and tend to think in legal terms. They frequently use language that is unintelligible to the average lay person and, because they lack practical business experience, communication can be difficult.

SUMMARY

The need to give credit is a fact of life for most small businesses, but credit is expensive, and a certain number of credit customers will not settle their bills. You shouldn't offer credit to just anyone who asks for it – check each applicant's creditworthiness, using an agency if necessary.

Accurate information about the credit side of your business is crucially important to your long-term survival. You need to know how long, on average, it takes to collect a debt, who the slow payers are, and why they take so long to settle their accounts.

Debt collecting is tedious, costly and may be emotionally unpleasant. Certain small debts can cost more to collect than their face values, so great efficiency in debt-collecting procedures is required.

Draft standard debt-collecting letters and never be afraid to use the phone. You can sell debts to a collection agency or even pass all your invoices to a credit factor. The latter will pay you a proportion of the face value of invoices in cash and then collect the full amounts owed. However, both these possibilities are expensive to implement.

If you possess unambiguous evidence of the existence of a debt and there are no complicating factors, such as alleged non-delivery of the goods, defective produce and so on, then legal action should be considered, especially if less than £1000 is involved.

The County court small claims procedure is very straightforward compared to normal litigation, although even here legal complications may arise. However, remember that there is no point in suing someone who does not have the means to settle an overdue account. Moreover, enforcement proceedings can be laborious and expensive.

✓ Checklist

☐ What proportion of your output is sold on credit?

☐ Suppose you were to insist on cash or cheques for all orders – what would happen to the level of your sales?

☐ How much are the discounts you offer for prompt payment actually costing you each year?

☐ Do you ask applicants for credit accounts to provide you with bankers' and other credit references?

☐ How long did it take you to collect the amounts owed for your last six credit invoices?

☐ Do you know the names and telephone extensions of the people who deal with suppliers' invoices in the accounts departments of your three largest customers?

☐ Have you ever telephoned a debt-collecting company to ask how much they charge? (Agency telephone numbers can be found in *Yellow Pages*.)

☐ Have you mentioned your debt-collecting problems to your bank and asked for advice?

☐ How many long overdue debts for amounts less than £1000 do you have on your books?

Notes

1. Re Peachdart Limited [1983] 3 WLR 878.
2. Notably the Consumer Credit Act 1974 (see Chapter 9).

Labour matters

INTRODUCTION

A good employee is one of the most valuable assets your business will ever possess; bad staff, conversely, can cause disaster.

You must be extremely cautious when recruiting, so interview carefully, then monitor the new entrant's work and regularly discuss problems that arise. It is not necessary to draft rigid job specifications for the employees of a small business or SME, because precise job descriptions invite 'who does what' disputes when, in fact, total job flexibility is usually needed.

There are of course, important legal constraints on how you recruit staff, but you will comply with the law provided you:

- do not discriminate unfairly on the grounds of race, sex or disability, or because someone is married;
- issue written contracts of employment and pay them what has been agreed on time;
- deduct the correct amounts of PAYE and Class 1 National Insurance contributions from employees' pay and turn these amounts over to the Inland Revenue at the end of each month;
- issue P60s at the end of each tax year.

FULL- OR PART-TIME EMPLOYEES?

Before you hire anyone, ask yourself, first, whether or not you really need to have 'employees' at all. The computation of PAYE and National Insurance is time-consuming and administratively troublesome, and all sorts of interpersonal relations problems may arise among employees. Perhaps you can subcontract work to other firms or possibly make do with part-time labour, which is much cheaper than hiring permanent, full-time employees.

Before you hire anyone, ask yourself, first, whether or not you really need to have 'employees' at all.

Note, however, that casuals may lack commitment, usually have less training and experience than full-timers, and may bitterly resent being employed on a casual rather than permanent basis, especially if they do the same work as better-paid full-time staff. This can result in low morale, frequent absenteeism and high staff turnover rates. Also, employees' grievances persist indefinitely among casual workers as complaints are passed on from one generation to the next.

If you employ full-time workers, then remember that they may not share your total loyalty to the business, which to them is probably (and understandably) little more than a means of earning a living. Employees may see you in a manner that is very different to how you see yourself. It is, after all, their hard work that will cause the business to succeed and they rightly feel entitled to a fair reward for their endeavours.

■ Small businesses and SMEs cannot afford idlers

There is no room for free-riders in a small firm or SME experiencing financial difficulties (or in any other business for that matter). Everyone must pull their weight and be willing to undertake whatever duties and changes in working practices are necessary to improve the business – no matter how personally inconvenient they happen to be. Ultimately, jobs depend on the long-term survival of the firm!

An advantage of working in a small business is that the employee has opportunities to experience a wide range of work activities. Jobs need not be as narrowly defined and specialised as is common in large organisations. All of these strengths should inspire staff to work hard.

EMPLOYEES WHO DON'T WORK HARD ENOUGH

Employees need not be overtly lazy before they start avoiding important duties – they might simply be trying, perhaps unintentionally, to exchange easier or more enjoyable duties for the tasks that really need to be done. Some jobs are necessarily less attractive than others and, not unnaturally, those who should perform unpleasant tasks may constantly seek alternative ways of filling their time.

An employee may be completely unaware of the extent of their task evasion. There is no question of deliberate malingering, yet nothing is achieved. Interesting duties are padded out to make them last longer, extra and unnecessary tasks are invented to run in parallel with jobs that are actually required and so the person becomes so busy completing these contrived duties that they have no time or energy left to deal with really important matters! Thus, the employee will:

- double-check documents;
- carefully peruse marginally relevant pieces of correspondence;
- investigate closely problems that have obvious solutions;
- query insignificant mistakes;
- ask for guidance on unimportant issues, and so on.

Sometimes employees behave like this because they wish to feel important and do not associate the mundane, lower-level duties you want them to perform with the status they believe they ought to command. Often, employees want to make decisions and have their own ideas about the decisions they should be allowed to make. Indeed, they have views about the entire distribution of work and responsibilities within the firm. These perceptions may differ from your own and so it is essential that you try to divide work between you and your employees in a manner that seems to them to be just.

HOW TO DEAL WITH A LAZY EMPLOYEE

A malingerer will minimise the effort they put into a job and attempt to shorten the length of the working day. Here, work avoidance is deliberate as the employee:

- is persistently late;
- takes unnecessary breaks;
- does walkabouts around the premises;
- tries to appear absorbed in tasks while actually doing nothing.

Of course, such individuals do some work just to avoid argument – files are shifted from one place to another, there are regular telephone calls to suppliers and other outsiders, and no shortage of conversation. Eventually, however, you realise that you are being ripped off. The employee wants the job, but is not prepared to expend any effort when undertaking the activities it involves.

The situation is intolerable as the employee is costing you money by the hour for very little return. Immediate and drastic measures are needed. Here's what you must do.

- Tell the person you think their work is unsatisfactory and why this is so. Specify detailed instances of unsatisfactory work, with dates, times and supporting documents where appropriate. Plan the discussion well in advance and never begin such an interview when you are tired, angry, upset or depressed.
- State that the discussion is more than just a 'friendly chat'; that you are seriously disturbed by the problems they are creating and that you intend to remedy the situation.
- Ask for comments and/or explanations. Are there mitigating circumstances (domestic problems causing frequent absences and coming in late, for example)?

> *You must, by law, give an employee 'reasonable' time to remedy deficiencies, and you must make crystal clear (preferably in writing) the standards you expect. Standards must be realistic, and the consequences of failing to achieve them explained fully.*

- Examine and question the reasons given for poor performance. Find out why the person has been malingering. If the employee denies everything, point to your evidence (which you must have collected prior to the discussion) of unsatisfactory work.
- Remind the employee of their responsibility to achieve a certain minimum standard and ask what you can do to help them overcome their current difficulties.
- Tell the individual that they should consider the interview as constituting a 'warning' about inadequate performance. Follow this up with a letter detailing your allegations, specifying occurrences and dates, and stating that if performance does not improve, then they may ultimately be dismissed.

You must, by law, give an employee 'reasonable' time to remedy deficiencies, and you must make crystal clear (preferably in writing) the standards you expect. Standards must be realistic, and the consequences of failing to achieve them explained fully. If the employee's work does not improve and they cannot advance any reasonable explanation for continuing to underperform then you have to repeat the above-mentioned procedure twice more. The second interview will be more pointed than the first, while the third should issue a final and unambiguous warning of dismissal.

All these discussions must be followed by letters confirming the warnings you have issued during the interviews. These letters should:

- point out that previous warnings were ignored;
- specify in detail further instances of incompetence or misbehaviour and mention that no satisfactory explanations or mitigating circumstances have been brought to your attention (but that if any exist you must be informed immediately).

Such actions are administratively troublesome, unpleasant and you may be tempted not to bother – simply firing the worker when the situation gets out of hand. However, you can end up losing a costly unfair dismissal case if you ignore the procedures described. The Government-funded Arbitration, Conciliation and Advisory Service (ACAS) publishes a Code of Practice entitled *Disciplinary and Other Procedures in Employment* (The Stationery Office), which sets out in detail the procedures you need to follow. Obtain a copy of this, read it and adapt its recommendations to your particular needs. Note that similar considerations apply to redundancy situations where existing workers (industrious and competent though they might be) cannot be retained for the simple reason that you no longer have any work for them to do.

REDUNDANCY

If you need to make someone redundant and they have worked for you for more than two years you have to offer them a redundancy payment.

The size of the payment depends on the age of the person and how long they have worked for the firm, subject to an upper limit, which varies from time to time. (Details of current rates are available from the office of your local Jobcentre.)

Redundancy applies to the job, not an employee. This means that you have no further work available of the type previously undertaken by the employee affected, and must not be confused with dismissal for incompetence or a similar reason. You are obliged by law to seek alternative work for anyone threatened with redundancy, give adequate warning (plus rasonable paid time off to look for another job) and must consult with the employee's trade union, if there is one.

■ Selecting people for redundancy

If you make one person redundant but not another, you have to be able to demonstrate that, in selecting them for redundancy you applied fair and objective criteria when making your choice. Hence, you must consider the length of service, capabilities, ages, qualifications and experience of all staff previously employed in the type of work that has disappeared, and should take into account each person's suitability for alternative employment within the business. You cannot lawfully declare one worker redundant while simultaneously hiring someone else to perform that person's work.

■ Who to retain

If most of your workforce has to go, keep a skeleton staff of people who are best able to face up to the challenge. Only retain flexible and energetic workers, but recognise that they will not want to stay for very long unless your firm's performance (and hence their security of tenure) improves rapidly.

Note that there is no presumption that younger or older employees will perform better in these circumstances – young people are perhaps more adaptable in fast-changing environments, but may lack the experience and commitment of older colleagues (especially those who will have difficulty in finding another job). Each retained worker can act as a cost centre in their own right, and be made accountable for specific business rescue activities.

■ Guarantee payments

Employees today are legally entitled to 'guarantee payments' for individual days when they are under contract to work, but no work is actually provided, Thus, you cannot simply lay someone off for the day without pay just because the firm is short of work.

DISMISSAL

Under the Employment Rights Act (1996), which also covers redundancy and guarantee payments, employees with more than two years' continuous full-time service have the right not to be 'unfairly' dismissed. This means you cannot fairly dismiss an employee covered by the Act unless that person is genuinely redundant or is guilty of 'gross' misconduct or demonstrably inadequate performance or unless you have some other 'substantial' reason for their dismissal.

Normally, you must give an employee notice (or payment in lieu), although dismissal without notice – known as 'summary' dismissal – is permissible provided the employee's behaviour makes it impossible for them to fulfil their contract. Examples would be persistent drunkenness, violence, abusiveness to customers, wilful disobedience or incompetence that immediately and directly damages the business.

Any employee you dismiss after they have completed two years' service with the firm is legally entitled to a written statement of your reasons for the dismissal.

■ Gross misconduct

The term 'misconduct' has no legal definition – each case must be considered individually. Theft and violence are obvious instances of gross misconduct, although it is up to you to prove that:

- the misconduct actually occurred;
- it detrimentally affected the work of the firm;
- you acted reasonably at all times.

■ Incapacity and inadequate performance

An employee may be fairly dismissed if they cannot complete their work satisfactorily and/or do not have the necessary qualifications for the job. Someone who is sick may be fairly dismissed on these grounds, subject to the sick leave agreed in the employee's contract of employment.

Always keep documentary evidence of the incompetence of any employees you intend to dismiss, and do not write glowing references for them prior to dismissal as such letters might subsequently be used in evidence against your allegations of inadequate performance.

■ Other substantial reasons

Other reasons for fair dismissal might include being rude to customers, 'organisational efficiency' (though the exact meaning of this must be established in each case), a temporary job coming to an end (provided the jobholder was told from the outset that the job was temporary) or if the continuation of a person's employment would cause you to break the law – for instance, by employing a driver who has lost their licence.

You are entitled to cooperation and obedience from those you employ, although the orders you give must be reasonable, legal and not involve dangerous working practices. Orders given must be covered by the employee's contract of employment, and dismissal for disobedience is 'fair' only if the failure to obey is 'wilful and significant'.

In any of the above circumstances, you cannot legally dismiss the individual until they have been warned both verbally and in writing (preferably several times) and given the chance to improve. Following dismissal, the person is legally entitled to a written statement of the reasons for their dismissal.

■ Automatically unfair dismissals

Certain dismissals are 'automatically' unfair as far as the law is concerned. Thus, if you:

- sack a pregnant woman just because she is pregnant;
- dismiss someone for joining or refusing to join a union;
- sack employees when a business changes hands;

then your actions will automatically be deemed unlawful.

Note that your behaviour short of sacking an employee can also lead to an unfair dismissal claim. Hence if you act so unreasonably towards an employee (say, by cutting their pay or lengthening their working day) that they feel there is no option but to quit, then the employee can allege that 'constructive' unfair dismissal has occurred.

■ What you stand to lose

Unfair dismissal cases are heard by three-person industrial tribunals, comprising a legally qualified chairperson plus two lay representatives. If you lose, you must pay compensation. This will consist of some or all of the following, according to circumstances:

- a basic award, depending on the employee's length of service;
- a compensatory award to cover loss of earnings and/or accumulated pension rights;
- an additional award, should you fail to comply with an order to reinstate them (these are extremely rare – only occurring in 1 per cent of claims);
- special awards (which can be considerable) if the dismissal is automatically unfair and you refuse to obey a tribunal order (again, these are extremely rare in practice – much rarer than additional awards).

Although there are upper limits on the amounts involved in the first, second and third above, and although the total compensation award by tribunals to employees who win their cases averages little more than a few thousand pounds, compensation can be substantial, and there are no upper limits at all if unfair sex or race discrimination is the cause of the dismissal.

Note that only those with the requisite lengths of continuous service may claim to have been 'unfairly' dismissed. (Note also the important fact that a series of renewable short-term contracts, issued one after another, builds up continuity of employment, just as if it were a single contract for a longer period.)

■ Wrongful dismissal

Actions for 'wrongful' dismissal are possible in an ordinary civil court, usually the County court. An employee with only a few days' service may claim to have been wrongfully (as opposed to 'unfairly') dismissed. The sacked person initiates a breach of contract action and sues for damages equal to the monetary loss incurred as a result of not receiving proper notice of dismissal,

RIGHTS OF EMPLOYEES

An important right conferred by the Employment Rights Act is the right of employees to receive a written contract of employment within eight weeks of starting work.

- the names of employer and employee;
- the date when employment began and the date when continuous employment began;
- pay, or method of calculating pay;
- intervals at which payment is made – weekly, monthly and so on;.
- terms and conditions relating to:
  - hours of work;
  - holiday pay, including the pay due on termination of employment;
  - sick pay;
  - pension scheme;
- the length of notice of termination the employee is obliged to give and entitled to receive;
- a note indicating the employee's right to join, or not to join, a trade union;
- a description of the manner in which an employee can seek redress of any grievance relating to their employment;
- the title of the job;
- a note showing whether or not any period of employment with another employer counts as part of the period of employment for notice purposes;
- for firms employing more than 20 people, reference to a document stating the disciplinary rules, and naming a person to whom the employee can apply (and by what method) if they are dissatisfied with a disciplinary decision;

- any collective agreements that directly affect terms and conditions;
- place(s) of work;
- for temporary jobs, how long the employment is expected to last;
- for employees working abroad, the period to be spent outside the
  UK, the currency they will be paid in, any additional benefits
  payable as a consequence of working abroad and the terms and
  conditions relating to the employee's return to the UK.

It is not necessary for the written statement to cover all these points
in detail – the employee may be directed to documents that are easily
accessible for the full particulars. These documents could include, for
example, pension scheme handbooks or copies of the works rules.
Employees must be informed in writing of any changes in conditions
not more than one month after the change has been made.

Contracts of employment are important because they establish the
existence of an obligation to pay employees in return for a predetermined amount of work. Breach of a contract of employment will, on
the one hand, provide the firm with grounds for fair dismissal and,
on the other, enable the employee to sue for pay they have not
received. The contract is the ultimate determinant of the work an
employee must do.

Apart from the period of notice specified in a contract of employment, certain minimum periods are imposed by law. The Employment Rights Act demands that at least a week's notice be given to an
employee with more than a month's, but less than two years' service
and an extra week's notice for each year of employment thereafter
(so that, for instance, a worker with 8 years' service is entitled to 8
weeks' notice) up to a maximum of 12 weeks.

■ Pregnancy and maternity

Under the Employment Rights Act 1996, all pregnant employees are
entitled to 14 weeks' maternity leave, irrespective of length of service. This may not begin until 11 weeks prior to the expected week
of childbirth, at the earliest. The woman has the legal right to return
to her original job at the end of the period. It is necessary for her to
give 21 days' notice of intention to take maternity leave, in writing

if the employer so wishes. If the employee decides to return to work before the end of the 14-week period, she has to give 7 days' notice. A woman with more than 6 months', but less than 2 years' service with the employer is entitled to remuneration from her employer at the rate of 90 per cent of her normal pay for 6 weeks, plus statutory maternity pay for a further 12 weeks. Pregnant employees with less than 6 months' service are not entitled to remuneration from their employers, although they will receive the appropriate amount of state benefit. It is (automatically) unlawful for an employer to dismiss an employee for being pregnant, having a child or taking maternity leave, even if the pregnancy makes her incapable of doing her job. In the latter case, the worker must be found alternative work or, if none is available, be 'suspended' on full pay.

A woman with more than two years' continuous service has extra rights. Such an employee will receive maternity pay at the standard rate for a period not exceeding 18 weeks, but if she has continued to work up to the eleventh week before the baby is due and has given her employer at least 3 weeks' written notice of absence, she will receive for the first 6 weeks of absence maternity pay at a higher rate – that is nine-tenths of her normal pay. After 6 weeks she will receive (for not more than 12 weeks) maternity pay at the standard rate.

■ Laws that prohibit discrimination

The Sex Discrimination Act 1975 aims to eliminate discrimination between men, women and married persons. Under the Act, it is generally unlawful for an employer to discriminate on grounds of sex or marriage in recruitment, in the terms and conditions of employment offered or in the provision of access to training or promotion opportunities. 'Direct' discrimination occurs when people are treated less favourably on account of their sex or because they are married. 'Indirect' discrimination means imposing a condition such that the proportion of members of one sex who can meet the condition is considerably smaller than it is for the other – such as a statement in a job advertisement that all applicants must be over six feet tall. 'Victimisation' results from people being less favourably treated because they complain of not receiving their statutory rights or because they help someone else complain of unfair treatment. There are several exceptions to the Act. These include:

- employment mainly outside Great Britain;
- employment in religious organisations that operate a sex bar;
- certain occupations (coal mining for example) where Parliament has decided women should not be employed;
- employment in the armed services.

Also exempt are jobs where sex is a 'genuine occupational qualification'. Examples are actors who play male or female roles, jobs in single-sex schools, hospitals or other institutions, and jobs where 'decency or privacy' require employees of a particular sex (lavatory attendants, for instance).

The Race Relations Act 1976 offers similar rights to minority ethnic groups. As with the Sex Discrimination Act, exemptions are available where race is a genuine occupational qualification.

Responsibility for seeking to eliminate racial discrimination in employment lies with the Commission for Racial Equality, which publishes codes of practice to guide firms in these respects. Similarly, the Equal Opportunities Commission issues codes of practice in relation to the avoidance of sex discrimination. Both Commissions conduct research and initiate legal action against firms that unlawfully discriminate.

■ Industrial tribunals and discrimination

Employees who believe they have been subject to sexual or racial discrimination or who wish to register complaints under a variety of other employment regulations and statutes (including health and safety and equal pay legislation), may initiate actions in industrial tribunals, the operation of which has been described in a previous section.

RECRUITING NEW STAFF

Aim for low-cost recruitment, avoiding, wherever possible, expensive press advertisements or recruitment agencies (which charge a fee of up to 10 per cent of the annual salary of the person eventually selected).

Word-of-mouth recruitment is cheap and highly effective in certain circumstances, particularly in areas of high unemployment. Put the word around that there are vacancies, supplementing this with a few letters to existing contacts within your industry, the local Jobcentre and, perhaps, local colleges. Simply putting a notice outside your premises or in a nearby shop window might be sufficient to attract the right person.

■ Interviewing

When interviewing, seek to identify in candidates the personal qualities your business needs most, and try not to be swayed by irrelevant, subjective criteria. Consider only the skills, qualifications and experience required for successful completion of the job, and do not hire someone simply because they are more like yourself than the other applicants. (Owning and running a small business usually requires talents that differ significantly from those needed for working for someone else and following their instructions.)

Prior to the interview, ask yourself the following two questions.

- What exactly do I want the appointed person to do?
- What are the personal characteristics that will enable an individual to perform this work successfully?

Relevant personal qualities might include:
- the ability to mix easily and get on with others (including customers, suppliers and/or other employees);
- possession of a certain technical skill;
- alertness and the ability to interpret complicated issues;
- the ability to withstand stress, cope with irate customers, work independently and so on;

plus whichever further attributes you deem appropriate for the job.

Prepare a checklist of these points for use in interviews, and consider how they can be assessed in candidates. Thus, for example, you might require a person who needs not be physically strong, but must possess good eyesight, has passed a certain technical examination, has a minimum amount of experience of a particular type of work and has already worked in a certain industry, who is emotionally stable, willing to work overtime and so on. You are unlikely to find anyone who matches this specification exactly, but at least you have some objective criteria against which to evaluate the people who apply.

■ Obtaining information

Use interviews to obtain information about candidates. Do not talk about yourself and your achievements. Avoid pomposity and do not ask aggressive questions that serve only to upset the candidate and interrupt the free flow of conversation. Act naturally when interviewing, remembering that the person you hire must work with you as you are, not as you transitorily appear during a half-hour discussion. Ask open-ended questions rather than those requiring simple 'yes/no' answers, and do not make insensitive remarks after an answer has been presented.

Try always to put the interviewee at ease. The more relaxed people feel, the more useful information they will transmit and the easier, therefore, will be your eventual choice of candidate.

Try always to put the interviewee at ease. Be polite, pleasant and sympathetic to their inevitable nervousness. Avoid keeping people waiting and make their reception friendly and constructive. The more relaxed people feel, the more useful information they will transmit and the easier, therefore, will be your eventual choice of candidate.

■ Applicants with criminal records

The law states that a 'rehabilitated' person does not have to disclose to a recruiting firm the fact that they have a criminal record, provided the applicant's conviction has been 'spent'. It is unlawful for an employer to deny someone a job solely on the grounds that the applicant has a spent conviction. If an applicant is asked to declare on an application form whether or not they have a criminal record or are questioned about this during an interview, the applicant is entitled to deny ever having been convicted of the spent offence.

A conviction becomes 'spent' following the elapse of a certain time period, although some convictions can never be spent (notably life sentences and other sentences of imprisonment of more than 30 months). Otherwise, the period involved varies according to the gravity of the offence. Thus, a prison sentence of up to 6 months becomes spent after 7 years; sentences of between 6 and 30 months are spent after 10 years; a probation order is spent 1 year after it expires, and so on. The periods are halved if the person involved was under 17 years of age when they were convicted.

There are exemptions to the legislation, and candidates for certain jobs do have to reveal past convictions. These jobs are lawyers, chartered accountants, medical practitioners, nurses, dentists, vets, prison officers, firearms dealers, social and health workers, and any form of work with children under the age of 18.

If a job applicant has a spent conviction that you know about, you must not reveal this information to anyone else as you could then be sued for defamation and/or the aggrieved person could make a formal complaint to the police, who might then prosecute you.

You may feel that this law is unfair on the grounds that you believe it necessary to ensure that everyone you hire is trustworthy and reliable. Remember, however, that a person's criminal record might have arisen many years previously and involve only a minor offence. Moreover, criminal records are held only by those who were caught and punished at the time. It is hardly proper that such individuals be punished again by not being able to get a job.

■ Beware of early resignations

Do not 'oversell' the job. Unfulfilled promises may lead to early disenchantment.

Be particularly on your guard when early resignations occur when you used an employment agency to make initial contact with the recruit. Most agencies offer a full refund if you sack a worker within a month of appointment, and a partial refund if the worker turns out to be unsatisfactory and, hence, is dismissed after a month but before the expiry of (usually) one year. Check the details of the contract offered by an agency to ensure similar provisions apply to staff resignations. Otherwise you might hire someone, pay a hefty agency fee, and then lose both the fee and the employee when they become dissatisfied and quit after a short period.

MOTIVATING YOUR EMPLOYEES

■ High staff turnover?

If workers remain with you, on average, for only short periods, you need to question the basic causes of their leaving. A high staff turnover is one of many indicators of flagging morale within the business. Other signs include:

- shoddy output;
- persistently late coming to work;
- frequent absenteeism;
- uncooperative and 'couldn't care less' attitudes.

Perhaps you are recruiting people to do work that is beyond them (extra training might solve this problem) or maybe you expect employees to achieve absurdly high targets or are starving workers of the resources necessary for them to perform effectively or possibly you have personal bad habits that cause employee dissatisfaction (such as regularly arriving for work after your employees have started, but always complaining if they do not turn up on time).

■ *Exit interviews*

Always ask people why they are resigning. Valid reasons include a better job elsewhere, lack of job security, moving house to another area, wanting more time to devote to young children and so on. Other, undesirable, reasons are boredom, personality clashes, frequent arguments with colleagues, lack of self-confidence, poor physical working conditions or marginally inadequate pay.

During the conversation, ask whether or not there is anything you can do to persuade them to stay, although explain that your purpose in conducting the interview is not to pressurise them into doing something they do not want to do, but, rather, to discover mistakes you have made in order to correct them and, hence, avoid their replacement being similarly affected. Encourage the worker to speak freely, express opinions, describe work experiences and state how they perceive the business and your behaviour as a good or bad employer.

■ How to motivate staff

Employees are motivated in part by the need to earn a living and in part by:

- psychological and social needs for job satisfaction;
- occupational dignity;
- job security.

As a small business or SME, you cannot offer your employees 'promotion' as such – indeed, even their job security might not be guaranteed. Nevertheless, you can:

- design jobs to generate the maximum amount of variety and interest for them;
- devise performance-related incentive schemes that enable you to give them decent pay without bankrupting the organisation.

■ *Job design*

Avoid giving employees single, repetitive and boring tasks that they have to complete for excessively long periods, and do not ask them to work in social isolation, spending all their time away from the company of other people. If the work to be done is necessarily monotonous, try to arrange the circumstances in which it is undertaken in such a way that the employee can easily communicate with others and can frequently enter into exchanges regarding various aspects of the routine job. Employees are usually better motivated if they personally control working methods and make significant decisions, since then they feel they have a personal stake in the survival of the business. Thus, wherever possible:

- combine single tasks into a composite whole;
- allow employees discretion about how they achieve objectives;

- make people responsible for the quality of their output;
- allocate them challenging duties that stretch their abilities.

Make jobs interesting

If you are to design jobs effectively, you need to know which aspects of the firm's work are least and most interesting – only then can you know what to do to make jobs more varied and absorbing from the employee's point of view. Hence, you should regularly experience the work yourself, and consciously analyse the factors that cause certain tasks to be boring. Then, perhaps, you can regroup activities, alter the pace of work, allocate broad rather than specific targets, encourage employees to participate in decision making and so on in order to improve interest and motivation.

> *If you are to design jobs effectively, you need to know which aspects of the firm's work are least and most interesting – only then can you know what to do to make jobs more varied and absorbing from the employee's point of view.*

Satisfied employees are easy to supervise – they are cooperative, productive and profitable. Sometimes people feel better if they have an impressive-sounding job title (especially if it incorporates the word 'manager') and there is no reason for a small firm or SME not to have employees with grandiose titles – 'chief accountant' for the part-time assistant who (among other things) does the books, 'head of marketing' for the person who takes customers' orders, and so on. Seek to compliment employees on the calibre of their work and, if you have to criticise, direct your remarks towards criticism of an action rather than an individual person. Try to involve staff with final customers – much satisfaction can be gained by observing a customer's pleasure in a high-quality finished product.

■ Incentive schemes

Few employees are prepared to accept piece-work pay without having a guaranteed fall-back minimum income. Unfortunately, you might not presently be in a position to offer employees the levels of pay they deserve and so need to devise some form of output-related remuneration package that nevertheless, contains, a guaranteed minimum level of earnings. Possibilities include:

- awarding higher rates to anyone who exceeds a predetermined target for output;
- output-related bonuses given in addition to basic pay;
- giving employees a certain proportion (say, half) of the money saved by completing a job early so that, for instance, an employee who completes in one hour a task that normally takes an hour and a half receives a bonus of a quarter of an hour's pay at their standard hourly rate.

Bonuses need to be:

- substantial – at least 10 per cent of basic pay – otherwise they offer no significant incentive;
- linked to quality or output levels that employees can themselves control;
- not too complicated or time-consuming to estimate.

▨ Profitsharing

Profitsharing is a further possibility, especially where individual contributions to output cannot be measured exactly. This may encourage employees' commitment to the business, although payouts are not directly connected to immediate effort so they might not associate the eventual payment with the hard work they put into its creation during a past period.

You must establish a criterion for allocating the profit to be distributed (such as, length of service, basic pay or whatever), and decide whether to pay the profit shares in cash or fringe benefits (which may, in fact, be extremely tax-efficient for the employees). Profitsharing will not motivate employees unless the amounts involved are substantial and seen as additions rather than alternatives to basic pay. A major problem here is that employees often come to regard profit distributions as integral parts of their normal incomes and so resent withdrawal of the benefits when the firm is passing through a rough trading period.

THE LAW ON HEALTH AND SAFETY AT WORK

The law on health and safety matters is complicated and voluminous. Currently, the most important statute is the Health and Safety at Work, etc. Act (HSWA) 1974, which imposes on employers a general duty to ensure so far as is 'reasonably practicable', the health and safety at work of all employees. Breach of this duty can lead to a criminal (rather than civil) prosecution. Any firm employing more than four workers must, under the Act, prepare a written statement of its policy on health and safety and bring this to the attention of employees. Plant, machinery and other equipment must be safe and well maintained, and all arrangements for handling, storing and transporting articles and substances must be safe and free of health hazards. Importantly, employers are obliged to provide the supervision, instruction and training needed to ensure health and safety. Firms are statutorily obliged to check that all aspects of the workplace are safe, including means of entry and exit, machinery and equipment and the working environment (fumes, dust and so on).

Section 7 of the Act states that employees must take 'reasonable care' to ensure they neither endanger themselves nor others at work. Thus, your employees are legally required to cooperate on health and safety matters, though note that it is your responsibility to ensure that instructions are carried out. For example, if protective clothing is necessary, then not only must you provide it, free of charge, but you must also make sure that it is worn.

■ Management of health and safety

A number of EU regulations on the management of health and safety at work came into force in 1993 requiring employers to undertake 'risk assessment exercises' intended to identify potential dangers to the health and safety of employees or anyone else likely to be affected by the firm's operations. The Management of Health and Safety at Work Regulations 1992, in particular, required that the risk assessment be completed by competent people (who may be outside consultants) and that, for firms with five or more employees, a permanent record of the exercise be maintained. In addition, the firm is obliged to:

- devise and implement specific procedures for dealing with emergencies;
- draw up a plan for putting into effect preventive and protective measures;
- train employees in safety matters and ensure that they are capable of avoiding risks – employees (including temporary workers) must be informed of risks in language that they can understand;
- take into account working conditions and local workplace hazards when selecting equipment;
- identify unavoidable risks in relation to handling operations, having regard to the shape, size and weight of the load and the ergonomic characteristics of the workplace (humidity, space available and so on).

■ Safety representatives

If you recognise a trade union, then, if it so wishes, it can appoint 'safety representatives' at the place of work. The union does not need your permission to do this, but it must be 'recognised' by you for the purpose of collective bargaining. Unions themselves decide the procedure for selecting safety representatives, whose functions include:

- investigation of hazards, accidents and dangerous occurrences, and making representations to management on matters arising from these investigations or on any other safety issue;
- meeting outside inspectors and receiving information from them;
- making formal inspections of the workplace every three months or following accidents or dangerous occurrences;
- inspecting and taking copies of any relevant information (accident reports, for example) that the employer is statutorily obliged to maintain.

■ Safety policy

Regardless of statutory and common law duties, you should always pay meticulous attention to health and safety matters. Do not be afraid of being accused of over-fastidiousness in these respects –

your good example is bound to influence others and, hence, reduce accidents in the longer term. Accidents are expensive. Not only do they disrupt production, but they also incur the costs of sick pay, investigations, training of temporary replacement employees and so on. Consciously seek to identify hazards and inculcate in others a respect for safe methods of work. Never authorise or even condone unsafe working practices. Try instead to incorporate safety checks into the systems and procedures of the firm. Be seen to investigate all accidents, and regularly inspect machinery and equipment. Insist on 'good housekeeping' within the business and that all accidents, no matter how trivial, be reported.

> *Regardless of statutory and common law duties, you should always pay meticulous attention to health and safety matters. Do not be afraid of being accused of over-fastidiousness in these respects – your good example is bound to influence others and, hence, reduce accidents in the longer term.*

■ Other safety legislation

Although the HSWA is intended as a piece of umbrella legislation that will eventually incorporate all other health and safety statutes, it does not replace existing health and safety laws, which continue to operate in parallel with it. The major statutes are outlined below.

■ *The Offices, Shops and Railway Premises Act 1963*

This Act applies to offices everywhere, even those on premises normally used for other purposes (factories, for example), although temporary offices or those operated for less than 21 hours a week are excluded.

Among the Act's major provisions are the requirements that:

- premises, furniture and fittings be kept clean, and that floors be washed weekly;
- each person should have at least 40 square foot of space;
- rooms be properly ventilated, lit and heated (that is, to at least 16 degrees centigrade after the first hour);
- washing facilities with hot water, soap and towels be provided, and that lavatories be accessible and properly maintained;
- no employee be expected to lift dangerously heavy weights;

- floor, passages and stairs be kept clear and safe, and that all dangerous machinery and equipment be guarded;
- first aid boxes be provided, the contents of which conform to the requirements of the Health and Safety (First Aid) Regulations 1981;
- seating must be available, and staff be given facilities for keeping clothing not worn at work.

The Fire Precautions Act 1971

The essential requirement of this Act is that certain classes of premises (including those covered by the Offices, Shops and Railway Premises Act (OSRPA) 1963, factories, and buildings to which the public has access) possess a 'fire certificate' issued by the local fire authority, which must be satisfied that the means of escape from the building and other fire precautions are adequate. Shop premises require a certificate if:

- more than 20 people are employed in the shop, or;
- more than 10 people are employed at any one time in an upstairs room.

Your firm should register its premises with the local fire authority, await an inspection and then adhere to the fire authority's advice. Over and above this, however, you should encourage your employees to be fire conscious and to remove fire risks. Ensure that all your staff know how to use fire appliances, the location of fire exits and how to operate the alarm system. Under the Act, staff must be given training in evacuation procedures and the use of fire-fighting equipment kept on the premises. Moreover, written records of all equipment, inspections and training sessions must be kept, stating the topics covered during the session, who supervised the session and who attended.

The Factories Act 1961

This contains similar provisions to the OSRPA, but for factories. However, additional regulations are included on the maintenance of hoists and lifts and, importantly, it specifies maximum working hours for young persons (restrictions on women's working hours were abolished in 1986), and that all young persons working in factories must be medically examined within two weeks of starting work. A firm may request exemption from the Act's restrictions on working hours for young persons if it needs to meet exceptional demand for output, provided the firm can demonstrate that adequate welfare facilities will be provided. Exemptions are not issued for more than one year.

■ Miscellaneous legislation

The Employers' Liability (Defective Equipment) Act 1969 provides that when an employee is injured because of a defect in the equipment provided by their employer and the defect is the fault of a third party (the equipment's manufacturer, for instance), then the injury is deemed to be also attributable to the negligence of the employer, even if no actual negligence has occurred. The employer can, of course, sue the third party for any loss suffered.

Under the Employer's Liability (Compulsory Insurance) Act 1969, every employer must insure against liability for bodily injury or disease sustained by employees in the course of their work, and a copy of the insurance certificate must be displayed on the premises.

Another important piece of legislation is the Occupier's Liability Act 1984, which requires the occupier of premises to take 'such care as in all the circumstances is reasonable to see that visitors will be reasonably safe in using the premises for the purpose for which they are invited by the occupier to be there'. Visitors are defined as persons on the premises for the benefit of the occupier (customers, for example), guests and those entering under contract.

Note that under the Unfair Contract Terms Act 1977, notices warning of dangers or hazards will not necessarily relieve an occupier from liability for injury to visitors. Thus, notices proclaiming that 'Persons entering these premises do so at their own risk' have no legal effect.

The Working Time Directive 1994 entitles employees to a daily rest of 11 consecutive hours in any 24-hour period; to rest breaks during any working day longer than 6 consecutive hours and a weekly rest period of 24 consecutive hours.

The maximum working week is restricted to 48 hours, although member states have the right to opt out from this provision until the year 2006, provided employees are legally permitted to refuse to work more than 48 hours without jeopardising their employment. Full-time employees can take three weeks' paid leave annually (four weeks after 1999). Under the Directive, night workers may not work more than 8 hours in any 24-hour period. They can also demand a free initial health assessment, plus regular medical check-ups thereafter. If night working causes an employee to experience health problems, then they should (wherever possible) be transferred to day work.

The EU Directive on the protection of young people 1996 establishes a minimum working age of 15 years (except in special circumstances) and requires that working conditions for employees aged between 15 and 18 be adapted to protect their physical, moral and social development.

Persons under 18 are prohibited from undertaking certain types of work, and risk assessments must be completed before young people commence employment. Also they must not work for more than 8 hours a day or 40 hours weekly; night work is heavily restricted. 'Working children' (that is, school students under 15 years of age who are undergoing work experience or training) must be given 14 hours' continuous rest in any 24-hour period. Other young workers under 18 must have at least 12 hours' continuous rest daily. All young people are entitled to two consecutive days' rest each week. A half hour break must be given after four and a half-hours' work.

VICARIOUS LIABILITY

Employees who make decisions that may be in breach of a statutory requirement or other legal obligation are normally (but not always) protected by the doctrine of 'vicarious liability'. This holds that if a person is an employee of an organisation, then their employer is liable for civil (but not criminal) wrongs committed in the course of the employee's employment, and not the employee personally. The phrase 'in the course of employment' means acts authorised by the employer or, where they are not formally authorised, where actions are so closely connected with employment that they are incidental to the employee's work. Only if an action is clearly outside the scope of employment will the employee be personally liable.

Thus, if an employee sacks a subordinate wrongfully, then it is the firm that might be sued rather than that individual. The same applies to negligence at work, with the exception of certain aspects of the law on health and safety, as the HSWA explicitly imposes a duty on all managers to take such steps 'as are reasonably practicable' to protect employees from injury. If an employee fails to take 'reasonably practicable' steps and, as a result, someone has an accident, then they could be personally liable.

Note that while it is technically possible for you to try and pass on to a negligent employee the losses you incur as a result of their negligence (say, by suing for damages), a court is unlikely to accept your claim. Moreover, the court will expect you:

- to have made explicit to the employee the fact that they would be exposing themselves to the possibility of such an action prior to the time the negligence occurred;
- to have paid the employee a pay increment specifically earmarked for the purpose of taking out insurance against this eventuality, and to have advised the employee of the intended use of the payment.

Much litigation has concerned the question of what exactly constitutes the 'course of employment' as:

- vicarious liability applies only to employees hired under a contract of services, and not to independent contractors (or self-employed consultants);
- employees must be doing what they are supposed to do (albeit carelessly, fraudulently or disobediently) at the moment the unlawful act occurs.

Note, however, that you are liable for acts committed by an independent contractor if you authorise them (perhaps indirectly) or order the contractor to do dangerous work. Also, many ambiguities surround the situations where:

- employees are using their own equipment or other property while pursuing the firm's business;
- an employee commits a crime that benefits the firm;
- an employee is mixing their own business with that of the employing organisation;
- employees take unauthorised action to protect the employer's interests (attacking would-be thieves, for instance), but commit offences while so doing – for example, by causing physical damage to other people or their property.

SUMMARY

A good employee is possibly the most valuable asset a small firm or SME can possess; a bad one could ruin the enterprise. You need therefore to take great care when recruiting and managing employees – never discriminate unfairly and always pay your staff in full and on time. Recognise that an employee might not be as committed to the business as yourself, but that they could still be a first-class worker. Generally, however, employees of small firms or SMEs are better motivated than those in large organisations because of the wide range of duties they are typically called on to perform and their close relationship with their bosses.

Occasionally, owners of small businesses or SMEs mistakenly hire employees who are lazy or incompetent. No small firm can survive in the long term if it employs indolent staff. If you find yourself in this position, you must grasp the nettle and confront the offending person, taking care not to violate current legislation on redundancy and dismissal.

Firms experiencing severe financial difficulties might need to consider making people redundant. Certain procedures must be followed when implementing redundancies. You must not discriminate unfairly when selecting the workers who are to go, and redundancy payments must be given to workers with more than two years' continuous service. Also, before declaring someone redundant, you are legally obliged to seek alternative work for that person.

Nowadays, you cannot sack someone simply because you do not like them – substantial reasons are necessary to support a fair dismissal. Normally, the burden of proving that a sacked employee was grossly incompetent, or misbehaved so badly that dismissal was justified will fall on you.

Dismissal of employees should always be avoided. Try, instead, to motivate them by giving thought to job design, delegation of interesting work and performance-related incentives.

There is much legislation concerning the rights of employees, especially in the fields of pregnancy and maternity leave and pay, working conditions and the health and safety of people at work. As the owner of a small business or SME, you need to be familiar with this legislation – at least in outline.

✓ Checklist

☐ How willing are your employees to undertake any job you give them rather than just the duties outlined in their formal (or informal) job specifications?

☐ Have you consciously tried to vary the range of tasks undertaken by your employees in order to make their jobs more interesting?

☐ Are your employees actually doing the types of work you originally hired them to do and, if not, why not?

☐ How much training has your workforce received during the last three months?

☐ How often do you delegate interesting managerial duties to your employees?

☐ Do you understand the procedures you must follow before dismissing someone?

☐ How much did it cost to recruit the last person you employed?

☐ When you interview job applicants, do you prepare a checklist of points to raise during the interview?

☐ Have you ever hired an employee who turned out to be totally unlike the person you expected following their recruitment interview? How do you explain the difference?

☐ What are the three most interesting jobs undertaken by each of your employees, and which are the three most boring?

☐ Can you honestly say you have done everything humanly possible to ensure the health and safety at work of your employees?

Selling your output

1
2
3
4
5
6
7
8
9
10
11
12

INTRODUCTION

Long-term survival requires regular reassessment of marketing methods, the incessant search for new markets and additional ways of attracting custom. This chapter discusses the process of marketing in general, leaving the specific techniques of low-budget advertising and sales promotion until Chapter 8, where they are dealt with in depth.

When you started the business, perhaps you assumed that, provided you offered a first-class product at a reasonable price, customers would fall over themselves to purchase your goods. While it is true that excellent and competitively priced output does help to sell itself, far more is required to achieve the maximum volume of sales for your product.

WHAT IS MARKETING?

Marketing is not the same as 'selling', although obviously an increased level of profitable sales is always the ultimate aim. Rather, 'marketing' is a whole range of activities:

- advertising
- packaging
- sales techniques
- public relations, sales promotions
- providing after-sales service
- deciding on prices
- planning and introducing new products

all of which complement each other and, hopefully, contribute to expanding your market share.

Try not to think of marketing as simply the process of finding customers for products or services you have already decided to supply. The output your firm produces may be of high quality, but it might not bewhat consumers wish to buy!

Questions you need to ask are as follows.

- Who is likely to purchase the product and why?

- What features does your output possess that are not available in competing products?
- Where are potential customers located and how best can you get through to them?
- What product attributes are most needed by consumers, to what extent and how does your output fulfil these needs? How high a price is the typical customer willing to pay?

Answer these questions frankly and comprehensively (resources permitting) and then gear your marketing efforts to supplying those products that best satisfy consumer needs.

Particular attention will have to be devoted to certain aspects of marketing, depending on the nature of your firm. If, for example, you produce consumer goods sold by retailers, then you may need to concentrate on:

- packaging;
- display and sales promotion;
- maintenance of favourable price differentials;
- devices for bringing the product to retailers' (as well as final consumers') attention.

If, conversely, you sell industrial goods through the trade, you might be better off focusing on trade advertising, on transport arrangements, after-sales service, image building or some other marketing activity that is especially relevant to your specific line of work.

A NEW MARKETING STRATEGY

It is essential that all links in the chain – from production of output to its final sale – operate efficiently and interrelate. Recognise, for instance, that advertising unsupported by a well-packaged product and an adequate distribution system is bound to fail eventually. Dispatch and transport arrangements should guarantee that goods are available to consumers on time, where and when required. At the far end of the chain, after-sales service, where

> *It is essential that all links in the chain – from production of output to its final sale – operate efficiently and interrelate.*

appropriate, should encourage repeat orders and generate recommendations to purchase your product to third parties.

The five major steps in formulating a marketing strategy in a small business are described below.

■ Positioning the product

This means:

- deciding how you want the customer to think of your product – as high-class, top end of the market (and expensive) output or as a 'cheap and cheerful' goods offering excellent value for money at a low price;
- taking appropriate measures to influence consumers' perceptions of the goods.

The decision has many implications – for product price, quality levels, selling methods, choice of distribution channel, promotional strategies and so on. In making the decision, think carefully about the state of market demand and how this might evolve. From which sources do you expect most new business to develop, and why? How easily can you create a 'brand image' (see below) that fits in with a top, middle or bottom end of the market position? Other relevant considerations include:

- production costs – and hence, feasible selling prices;
- the extent and quality of competition in various market segments;
- specific features of the product, its selling points and to which types of consumer these are likely to appeal.

■ Targeting the customer

What type of person is most likely to buy your firm's output? Specify the target consumer's age, sex, income, social class, family size and situation, social habits and geographical location. Other 'market segmentation' variables that could be relevant include religion, marital status, political orientation and nationality, plus any other criterion you feel might be important for marketing the product.

Gear your products and their presentation to the particular needs of various target segments. This might involve changing product names in order to enhance their appeal to certain consumer types or altering colours, order sizes, packages, specifications or perhaps even the product price.

Efficient customer targeting is essential for small businesses and SMEs. You must identify the subgroups that constitute the total market for your output and then vary the features of your product(s) in order to make them attractive to the most lucrative market segments. Note that different advertising media and messages will normally be appropriate for each part of the market.

Analysing market segments

Aim to distinguish specific consumer groups (for example, high-income, middle-aged women with no children living at home, who work in offices, have received a certain level of education and who cook using electricity) within which potential customers are as homogeneous as possible. Then, devise advertisements and sales promotions (see Chapter 8),

> *Accurate segmentation enables you to pinpoint selling opportunities and tailor your marketing activities to satisfy consumer demand.*

and select styles, prices, packaging designs, quantities and quality levels that are particularly suitable for those markets.

Frequently, it is more profitable to supply a large share of each of a small number of niches in a big market than to spend lots of money gaining just a small share of the wider market. Accurate segmentation enables you to pinpoint selling opportunities and tailor your marketing activities to satisfy consumer demand.

Consumer lifestyles

Once you have identified a possible market segment in terms of the previously mentioned variables, write out a brief account of the typical lifestyle of a member of that particular group. Imagine you are that person and ask yourself the following questions.

- What do they do on a typical day, from rising in the morning to going to bed at night?
- What are this individual's opinions and prejudices on various issues?

- To which kind of lifestyle do they aspire?

Answers to these questions help determine the forms of advertising and promotional messages most suitable for reaching target groups. Consumers often select goods that correspond to their perceptions of what they should purchase in order to follow chosen lifestyles (or lifestyles to which they aspire) rather than to satisfy an objective physical requirement. Identify the lifestyle involved and you can present your product(s) in appropriate ways.

■ Selecting a price

Pricing is difficult because it not only requires the estimation of the costs of supplying products (which itself is problematical in view of the numerous ways you can allocate overheads), but also that you consider the effects of the chosen price on the image of your output. If your product is similar to products already being sold, then you will normally use the established 'market price' for that product type to guide your pricing decision. Otherwise, you have to consider consumers' perceptions of the quality of the product, its 'desirability' and how easily it satisfies their particular needs.

People sometimes judge the worth of an item by its price. They may assume that a very low price means shoddy output, regardless of what is objectively the case. Also, packaging can significantly affect the feasibilities of various pricing options. High-priced goods in low-grade cartons, for example, could destroy a product's credibility in consumers' eyes.

Expensive packaging can repay its initial costs several times. Consumers today demand packages that are aesthetically pleasing as well as functionally convenient. They want packages that:

- are easy to open, pour and reseal;
- have adequate instructions;
- are durable, disposable and so on.

If your output is currently sold loose or in the cheapest possible containers, then seriously consider the potential price rise benefits (that is, the ability to raise the selling price) that appealing packaging may provide.

■ *Skimming the market*

If target consumers are affluent, innovative, well-informed and edu-
cated, then consider adopting a high-price approach in order to 'skim
the cream' off the top end of the market. Here you offer an expensive
but high-quality and well-presented item with 'all the trimmings'.
Quality images are essential for this to work and there has to be a sufficient number of high-income consumers ready to pay top prices.

However, you can earn big profits if you adopt this strategy, provided supply costs are relatively low. Note, however, that other firms
will be attracted to the top end of the market if you are too conspicuous in your success.

■ *Penetrating new sectors*

Alternatively, low 'penetration' prices might be best for your business. These involve aggressive advertising and sales promotions in
conjunction with visibly low prices that aim to increase your firm's
share of particular market segments. The strategy is suitable where
bigger outputs enable you to reduce unit supply costs by bulk purchasing (at discount) of raw materials and other input supplies, integration of processes, making the fullest possible use of machines
and labour and so on.

Low-price policies will not succeed, however, if your competitors
drop their prices in line with yours, as then your market share
remains constant even though your revenues are reduced because of
the price cut. Also, the low price may cause customers to believe that
you are selling inferior output.

Other methods for determining prices include the following.

- Setting a target level of profit for the coming year, estimating how
  much you can sell and then pricing output in order to achieve the
  stated profit objective.
- Charging high prices when introducing new products and systematically lowering them thereafter. Here you attempt to recover
  start-up and development costs immediately following the launch
  of a new product, but recognise the need to lower the price as
  competitors emerge and in order to reach wider market segments.

- Selling certain items at less than their production or procurement costs to attract custom for other, higher-priced products, by means of which losses are recovered. (This practice is sometimes referred to as 'loss leading'.)
- Varying prices according to the state of trade. When order books are full, you raise output prices, then cut them when spare capacity occurs. This can damage your business eventually as customers frequently resent being charged different prices for the same goods at different times.

No outsider can definitively state what the best price policy for your firm is. This depends on circumstances, though, in choosing, much hinges on the product's unique selling points. Unless there is some particular reason to do so, consumers will not normally buy highly priced goods that are considered to be identical to competing products offered at lower prices. The existence of selling points will substantially determine the responsiveness of consumer demand to changes in price.

■ Selecting promotional methods

Whatever your line of business, you need devices to attract attention to your products, business and the fact that the firm is alive and well. Advertising is obviously important; so too are special promotions – coupons, competitions, distribution of free samples, premium offers (that is, where you offer a larger quantity for the same price or a free gift or cut-price item following the receipt of so many proofs of purchase) and so on. Such promotions can achieve several objectives. In particular, they can:

- increase sales – via stimulation of impulse and repeat purchases;
- enhance consumers' knowledge and awareness of products;
- gain retailers' goodwill and encourage them to display your firm's goods prominently;
- help fight off competition.

Promotions should be 'genuine', in the sense that they represent value for money in consumers' minds, yet they must not be too costly to implement! They will not usually arrest declining sales of existing and 'tired' products that have been on the market for some time unless you simultaneously repackage, redesign and/or improve the product by adding new features or selling points in some way. Promotions, moreover, have only a temporary effect on sales, which are short-lived and useful only for achieving immediate tactical goals. Yet, they may be just what is needed to generate extra sales when you experience deficits in short-term cash flow.

Reasonable intervals must elapse between promotions, and they should reinforce and complement the more general advertising you undertake. Remember that promotions cost money as extra quantities, special price cuts, free samples and so on all have to be paid for, so budget carefully and plan your promotions well ahead. Good promotions are those that:

- are cheap and simple to administer;
- do not involve your giving away too much.

You should test your promotions on a small scale before applying them marketwide in order to assess responses and, hence, forecast aggregate net returns. So important are sales promotions to the small business that they are considered separately in Chapter 8.

■ Choosing products

Think of a 'product' as anything the business might be able to sell, not just as a physical object or service. A window cleaner, for example, can offer several products for sale, albeit using the same bucket and cleaning leather. There are window cleaners who specialise in high-rise buildings, those who will only do domestic households, some who give generous discounts for shop and office window-cleaning work and so on. Certain window cleaners provide ancillary services, such as waste disposal, minor repairs, drainpipe and gutter clearing and so on, all of which provide unique selling points to the firm.

A window cleaner could operate under an evocative business name. A brief look at *Roget's Thesaurus* reveals some words and phrases that might be included in the firm's title – wipe-clean, bright and shiny, spit and polish, spotless, stain-free, plus many others. Use of an eye-catching business name ('Bright 'n' Shiny', for example), together with a mention of particular selling points (such as the provision of certain supplementary services and/or easy payment terms), creates a unique 'product' in consumers' eyes.

Product choice and development are crucially important in the overall strategy of your firm and are thus worthy of further attention.

PRODUCT CHOICE AND BUSINESS STRATEGY

What business are you in? The answer to this seemingly banal question is not as obvious as it might appear. For example, is a window cleaner in the glass washing business, hygiene, maintenance and repairs; appearance enhancement business or what? Alternatively, consider a building firm that can move into several alternative (and perhaps mutually exclusive) lines of activity – house repairs, roofing, shopfitting, the building of new houses, maintenance of buildings, dry rot and timber treatment and so on. Each option requires a somewhat different approach to marketing, specific advertising media, differing raw materials input, employee skills and so on. If you manufacture and/or sell stationery, are you in the paper business or graphic design or the written communications business? Suppose you repair mechanical products – do you restrict your activities to repairing metal and plastic objects or do you start learning about electronics in order to be able to repair electrical and information technology-related products (such as word processors or computer printers) as well?

■ The scope of your business

In answering these questions, you determine the scope of your business, its orientation and its style. The stationer, for instance, might conclude that their firm is in the office communications business and is not concerned merely with the purchase, processing and resale of paper. In this case, they will become interested in all aspects of office communications and related equipment – photocopying methods and systems, telephone equipment, e-mail, computer software, dictating machines and, indeed, anything to do with office communications. The product range of this firm will differ markedly from that of a stationer who simply designs letterheads and prints and sells various packaging materials and qualities of paper.

Are you in a fit shape to tackle the most lucrative of the available market opportunities and if not why not, and what must be done to remedy the situation?

■ Selecting activities

To select your range of products and activities, examine carefully the profitabilities of various market segments, their possibilities for further expansion and the ease with which new markets may be entered. Then list – honestly and comprehensively – your firm's particular strengths and weaknesses as they relate to these markets. Are you in a fit shape to tackle the most lucrative of the available market opportunities and if not why not, and what must be done to remedy the situation? Essentially, you have to choose between:

- concentrating on activities you know from experience you can do really well;
- initiating new products in completely new areas.

This choice – which amounts, in effect, to your answering the question 'What business should you be in? – can be extremely difficult. If you opt to carry on with your current activities you implicitly assume that you will be able to continue to undertake existing lines of work without hindrance, interruptions in supplies, predatory actions by competitors, equipment failures, strikes among distributors and so on, and that unexpected technological innovations will not render your product, or means of creating it, technically obsolete.

Seeking out new and entirely different business opportunities requires that profitable openings be available and that you possess the means for identifying their locations. Research is necessary and you must constantly assume risk.

Answering the following questions might help you to make the correct decision.

- How fast is the pace of technical change in the industry in which you operate and how easily can you match your rivals in the technical field? Unexpected technical change can put you out of business, so consider carefully whether or not long-term investment in capital equipment in a rapidly changing, high-tech industry is really worth while. Perhaps alternative, less technologically sensitive niches more suitable for you are available.

- How does your output differ from that of competitors, and what must you do to take full advantage of these differences?
- How safe is the firm's access to continuing supplies of the raw materials and other inputs needed to continue its present activities?
- Is it possible to improve existing products. If not, why not, and how would the introduction of a new, competing product affect your firm?

Products, however selected, should be branded. This applies to even the smallest of small firms (including the single-person, single-product business, such as a window cleaner or self-employed motor mechanic working from home).

BRANDING YOUR OUTPUT

Branding means giving a particular trade name or logo to your product(s) and then seeking by means of advertising and other promotional methods to associate certain attractive characteristics with the branded goods. This enables customers to recognise your goods. Having once purchased one of your products and been satisfied with it, the customer need not re-evaluate its worth prior to buying it again – they can choose a brand that is already known and trusted! For example, people buy Tippex, not whitener or correction fluid, as the brand name has become synonymous with the product.

Having created a branded product, your advertising and other promotions may then be directed towards establishing 'brand loyalty' via the reinforcement of existing favourable images. People will immediately identify the branded product – you need not provide fresh information about it in each and every advertisement.

■ Logos

Business logos are perhaps the commonest means of branding outputs. Either you can design your own logo or commission one from a local printer (most printers keep stocks of 'standard' logotypes that they adapt and cannibalise to meet specific customer needs). The logo might relate to your name or initials or consist merely of a distinctive symbol unconnected with the business (a drawing of a certain species of bird or animal, for example). Your logo should be shaped, lettered or coloured in a form that attracts attention and projects a favourable image of the firm.

■ The importance of branding

Note that neglecting to brand your product(s) can mean that much of your advertising is wasted. Suppose, for instance, that you operate a one-person window-cleaning service and decide to leaflet an area to advertise your firm. If you head the leaflet with the words 'Window Cleaning' or a similarly mundane title, you might simply remind householders to use the services of other local window cleaners. In effect, you are advertising partly for the benefit of your competitors.

Instead, you must particularise your specific offer of service by itemising the product's selling points (low price, no smear guarantees, money back if the customer is dissatisfied, special discounts for longer-term contracts and so on) and relating these to a clearly identifiable brand image embodied in an attractive and distinctive logo and other symbols of the firm.

■ Building in a brand image

Successful branding normally requires that products retain their unique brand identity right up to the moment of sale. Hence, brand names and logos must be securely attached (preferably built in) to your output. Otherwise, mixing up or repackaging of products by distributors or retailers may render your goods indistinguishable from other brands – the final customer is denied the opportunity to consciously select your output. There are exceptions to this rule, however. For example, where you supply goods knowing that they will be sold under someone else's label or name. Thus, a shirt (or other garment) dealer typically purchases shirts from several different manufacturers but sells them all under the dealer's own name.

■ Family brands

Brand images encapsulate whole collections of product attributes and special features. Consumers come to know what the brand represents and may thus satisfy their requirements without careful thought or research. They can also avoid repurchasing unsatisfactory branded items. If you sell several products, you must choose whether or not to allocate separate brand names to individual products or establish a generic 'family' brand covering all your output.

■ *Advantages of family brands*

The latter approach can be highly cost-effective, especially if the various products are closely related in people's minds because they are used together (toiletries, for example) or a common channel of distribution, a common customer group or similarity of prices. This is because the entire product range may then be advertised jointly under a single brand name, thus cutting the cost of advertising individual brands separately. Moreover, additions to product lines are introduced easily and inexpensively as no extra advertising or promotions need be incurred. The new product is simply incorporated into existing advertising literature – you do not have to establish a completely new individual brand image. Separate brands are essential, nevertheless, if you wish to appeal to different market segments or where products are markedly dissimilar.

Once a brand has been brought to customers' attention, selling costs diminish because:

- advertising attracts custom to your own brand rather than to that class of product generally;
- distributors and retailers are more willing to handle your goods on account of known demand for your particular branded output.

Branding contributes to the general image of your firm. Image building is an important aspect of marketing, worthy of separate attention.

THE IMAGE OF YOUR BUSINESS

We need to distinguish carefully between your business' image – that is, the mental impression it projects to outsiders – and the 'identity' of the firm, which serves to create the image. A firm's identity is visually recognised by means of:

- letterheads
- logo
- fascia of the premises
- typography of leaflets
- price lists and brochures
- the manner and dress of its owner and employees
- layout and style of the reception area
- tone of the person answering telephone calls
- name display and so on.

These are the physical manifestations of the business that generate its image to the external world.

Outsiders base their image of the business on their awareness of its identity and on direct experience of the firm's activities and behaviour. Thus, you should always be concerned that the various aspects of your business' identity (name, letterheads and so on) are congruent and generate a favourable image of innovation, quality, dynamism, reliability, success or other desirable attributes.

> *Your business name is important because it contributes significantly to the general image your firm creates, and, in particular, to customers' perceptions of the quality of your products.*

■ Your business name

Your business name is important because it contributes significantly to the general image your firm creates, and, in particular, to customers' perceptions of the quality of your products. It is no longer necessary to register a business name and provided:

- you do not imply you are connected with the government or a local authority;

- your business name does not include words prohibited by the Board of Trade (which publishes a pamphlet listing prohibited words);
- you give your own name and address on all business documents;

you can choose whatever business name you desire. If you trade under your family name or if the existing name of the business is dull and uninspiring, you should seriously consider how it could be altered. Thus, for example, 'Bright 'n' Shiny' sounds much better than 'R Bennett: Window Cleaner'; 'RHA Management Consultancy Limited' is a more impressive letterhead than the name and address of an individual person.

■ The persona of your firm

Like it or not, your business has several 'audiences' – customers, bank managers, suppliers, local authority trading standards officers, community neighbours, employees – that you need to impress and who will respond, albeit unconsciously, to the aura of the firm. The outward disposition your business projects will create thoughts about and feelings towards the firm that will encourage outsiders to behave positively or negatively when dealing with the business, without their necessarily being fully aware of why this is so.

■ Names and images

Certain words in a business name possess favourable connotations and imply high standards (reliability, honesty, integrity, sound after-sales service and so on). Search for words that relate to the theme of your business. The conventional *Roget's Thesaurus* (which is based on ideas and concepts rather than listing words alphabetically) is better for these purposes than more recent variations of it. Note, too, how positive images are sometimes best projected by means of motifs, logos and other visual means (multicoloured letterheads, for instance). People often intuitively understand the messages embodied in visual representations better than they do when they are written in words, so well-designed and printed letterheads, leaflets and brochures are essential ingredients of the promotional mix.

■ The need for a professional approach

Visit local printers and inspect samples of their work. Printers are pleased to offer advice and suggest logos and other designs suitable for your line of business. It is essential to realise that consumers today are immersed in professionally created advertising messages, and so they will assume that all firms – even small ones – will wish to project themselves as favourably as possible. Consumers (and others) may thus be extremely suspicious of a business that does not bother to display itself in attractive ways. To ignore external appearances is to invite people to perceive the firm as having 'couldn't-care-less' attitudes and being shabby and unreliable even though this may be far from true.

■ Selecting an image

Great care is needed when selecting an image because techniques for projecting one type of image might not be appropriate for projecting others and, once established, an image may be extremely difficult to change. The first important decision is which of the firm's potential activities to emphasise and which to leave out as the business' name, letterheads and other promotional material cannot possibly encompass all potential market opportunities. For example, if a small business or SME's target customers (householders) wish to replace some guttering or have other relatively minor repairs completed, they will be put off approaching this firm if it has created for itself an image of being concerned mostly with large-scale house extensions or major shopfitting. A business that is technically excellent can fail by having the wrong image. Impressions of ability can be as important for winning orders as actual competence in producing and delivering goods.

PUBLIC RELATIONS

Public relations (PR) is about creating and maintaining feelings of goodwill towards the business among outsiders. The resources available for this within a small business or SME are necessarily limited, although much useful PR can, in fact, be undertaken at low cost.

The first and most obvious possibility is the press release that you write yourself (in not more than 150 words) for circulation to local newspapers, including the ever-increasing number of free local papers distributed door to door. Very many items in local papers, especially giveaway papers, originate in press releases issued by local firms. Suitable topics for a press release include:

- a grand reopening;
- the launch of a new product or service;
- a change of name, plus details of the new orientation of the business;
- a personal achievement;
- your first major order;
- unusual uses for the product;
- a contribution to community affairs, such as job creation;
- a visit from a well-known personality.

Mundane news items do not appear in newspapers by accident – someone has taken the initiative to put them there. If you doubt the relevance of business news to local papers, just look through next week's issues and count how many brief items refer to local businesses or products. Most of these paragraphs will have begun as a press release.

■ Writing a press release

Even a minor modification to an existing product can be made 'newsworthy' by presenting it in certain ways. Thus, when announcing the modification you could describe:

- how it improves the goods or service you offer;
- its low cost and instant availability;
- how favourably it compares with other products, especially if safety is involved;
- what gave you the idea for the modification;
- its usefulness to particular consumer groups;
- discounts available and so on.

Always include details of where and how the product can be bought.

Write a release in the style of the paper in which you want it to appear and detail:

- what is happening;
- who is involved;
- where an event is taking place;
- when it is taking place;
- why the event is important.

You need an eye-catching headline that instantly identifies what the item is about and body copy that justifies the newsworthiness of the story. The subject should be specified in the first few words. Put the most important information first (often, only the first couple of paragraphs of a press release is printed) and be careful not to make the release read like an ordinary advertisement. Avoid technical jargon and unusual abbreviations throughout.

Photographs – interesting, 'newsworthy' pictures – can cause editors to accept items they would otherwise reject. Illustrations must be sharp to enable them to be reproduced well, and send in large prints of photographs to give the editor the option of 'cropping' them as required. Offer captions to accompany each photograph. Find some samples in your local paper and use them as a guide.

■ Other low-cost PR activities

Here are some other low-cost PR activities you can undertake.

- Arrange a reception to relaunch your business in a new format, and invite the desk editors of local newspapers, neighbouring businesses, major suppliers and leading customers to attend. Issue a press release to the journalists who turn up (and they will turn up if there is free food and wine) and get their telephone numbers for further PR work.
- Organise a display of your products/sales literature in the entrance to another business (offering them a fee for this) that services a lot of passing trade.
- Sponsor a local charity and ask it to issue a press release announcing your support.

- Make your premises available to local charities for their own press conferences and other media relations exercises (photo-call sessions, for instance).
- Have some T-shirts printed with your business name and give these away or sell them at low cost to customers and visitors to the firm.
- If you live in a densely populated area containing non-English speaking minority ethnic, contact the local ethnic language newspapers (these may possibly be little more than broadsheets or monthly newsletters) that cater for those groups and invite the editors to do special features on your firm. Offer a special discount to readers of these newspapers on presentation of a coupon that was printed in the papers involved.

SELLING FACE TO FACE

You do not need academic qualifications to be good at selling, but you must be able to see things from other people's points of view and identify and understand their requirements. Effective sales people are those who are capable of sensing customers' perceptions of their needs and convincing customers that a certain product will satisfy particular wants.

A typical sale can be broken down into stages as follows.

■ Contacting the customer

Gather as much information about the prospective customer as you can before making contact. If the prospect is a firm, find out about its products, organisation, key personnel, future plans and prospects. In the case where customers are members of the public who visit your premises, acquaint yourself with the type of person that is likely to enter the showroom or other selling area, so that you can avoid making introductory remarks that might offend potential customers. The aim of the initial introduction is to establish a comfortable relationship with the prospect that is based on mutual agreement, avoiding dissent wherever possible. Thus, casual observations about the weather, transport, sport and so on are generally preferable to contentious statements.

■ Arousing interest

Now engage the prospect in conversation. Seek to discover as much as you can about their special requirements. The customer will talk to you easily, provided you were able to establish an amicable relationship in your initial comments. Aim at this stage to increase the customer's awareness of the selling points of the product.

■ Presenting the product

The next objective is to form in the customer's mind a distinct preference for your goods in comparison with competitors' products. Where appropriate, demonstrate the product or illustrate its use with photographs, sales literature and, perhaps, a glossy brochure. Systematically increase the amount of product information presented. Explain how various aspects of the product satisfy the customer's particular needs. List the attributes of the product – its performance characteristics, reliability, quality, aesthetic appeal and so on. Describe how your firm will meet the consumer's requirements better than competitors – how you offer quick delivery, money back guarantees, technical advice, after-sales service, special discounts and so on.

■ Dealing with objections

Inevitably, the customer will experience misgivings and raise objections to your characterisation of the product. Treat objections as opportunities for exerting even more pressure on the customer (a frequently used rule of thumb is to answer each objection with three further benefits associated with the product). In order to have enough arguments ready to produce at the appropriate moment, you must hold back some selling points during earlier stages.

Often, the main objection is the high price of the goods. In response, aim to 'particularise' the item with respect to its unique features. Encourage the customer to think that this product has unique attributes not possessed by any other. A consumer who is convinced there is no comparable substitute for the product offered will not make mental comparisons of its price with the prices of competing items.

153

■ Closing the sale

Assume the customer has decided to buy, and phrase closing remarks accordingly. Questions such as 'Which colour do you want?' or 'When would you like us to deliver?' can prompt positive responses. If, despite all your efforts, the prospect still refuses to buy, be sure you leave on friendly terms – they might consider purchasing the product later.

Maintain detailed records on the numbers and values of sales achieved relative to the number of enquiries and contacts in various sales categories. Establish a reminder system for repeat follow-up calls and recording the outcomes of calls. Analyse all your sales extremely carefully. Prepare a form for completion after every contact itemising:

- the source of the enquiry;
- whether it was repeat or new business;
- time spent with the customer;
- whether or not a follow-up is likely to prove worth while;
- method of approach technical or personal emphasis, how familiar you were with the customer, any sales technique you consciously applied and the customer's response to it and so on;
- value of the order;

plus any other details particularly relevant to your products and line of work. Did the prospects you initially thought most promising actually convert into sales? If not, why not?

■ Analyse your effectiveness

Analyse the time you devote to face-to-face selling. How much time is spent in travelling and administration relative to time spent making a sale? Other matters worthy of investigation include:

- selling costs per sale and per customer;
- the value of discounts necessary to attract custom in various market segments;
- changes in the ratio of enquiries to sales.

The latter is worthy of detailed attention because if this can be reduced (say from five to one to four to one), the effect on sales is phenomenal.

Consider the feasibility of doing a telephone survey among those potential customers who enquired about your product(s) but who did not actually buy to discover the reasons for their deciding not to purchase. The cost of this exercise might be recovered several times over in the longer term because of the information it generates on your promotional/distribution inadequacies. And you might even pick up a few orders from the people included in the survey.

■ Lost customers

The loss of existing customers is especially disturbing, and each major loss should be analysed in depth. How easy was it for the customer to change their source of supply (you should always try to have customers 'locked in' to your products with long-term contracts and trade deals so that they gear their production or distribution systems to supplies of your goods), and why do you think the customers abandoned your business? Do not be afraid to ask customers for this information – you have nothing to lose.

■ *What went wrong?*

Where did you find the customer in the first instance? Can a replacement customer be obtained from the same source? Perhaps the customer is experiencing cash flow problems and is thus seeking a cheaper, albeit inferior, alternative to your product. Consider the feasibility of offering a special price in exchange for a long-term contract (though avoid giving credit) if this is so. Check to ensure that you provided the back-up, maintenance and after-sales service you promised in the contract.

■ How profitable are your sales?

It is vital that you analyse sales according to their contributions to profit as well as to sales volume. Small-value orders, for example, while perhaps contributing little to aggregate sales, might contribute a lot to total profits. Equally, very small orders might not be worth servicing. Either way, you need to know the exact position.

The bulk of your profits might be derived from just a few orders. If so, ask why this situation exists and seek to apply the factors contributing to high mark-ups to the less profitable of your sales. Many considerations explain differences in unit profitability:

- selling costs;
- packaging and delivery charges;
- method of distribution – mail order versus personal sale, for example;
- cash or credit settlement;
- discounts given on various order sizes;
- administrative costs and so on.

The frequency of delivery of supplies appertaining to a large order – such as twice rather than three times a week – can make a big difference to its profitability.

■ Develop your skills

Work hard at your selling skills – there will always be new things for you to learn. Keep notes on your selling successes and failures, with statements of why you succeeded or failed in particular instances. Experiment with various styles of dress and modes of behaviour (relaxed, assertive, formal, familiar and so on) until you find the one that works best for you. Enter selling situations in a positive frame of mind, determined to achieve a sale. Be friendly, sincere and respectful. Make sure you are fully briefed and, unless there are special reasons for not doing so, acquire a comprehensive technical knowledge of the product(s) sold by your firm.

TELEPHONE SALES

Where appropriate, experiment with telephone sales. This is a useful way to follow up customer enquiries, and enormous amounts of time and travelling expenses are saved if it succeeds.

Plan the telephone call carefully, specifying the objective you hope to achieve and the major points to be made during the conversation. Have all the relevant information before you prior to the call. Be brief, keep to the point and, if the prospect responds in a hostile manner, simply apologise for disturbing them and ask if you can ring again at a more convenient time.

RESEARCH

Marketing research is problematical even for the very large firm, let alone for the small business or SME, which does not possess the resources necessary for major investigations. Difficulties arise from environmental uncertainties and from the simple fact that human behaviour can and does change suddenly and unpredictably. Ideally, you should:

- test market new products before introducing them to the market as a whole;
- assess the psychological impact of your business image and advertisements on consumers;
- statistically, forecast the effects of a price change on sales and revenues and so on.

In reality, however, such aspirations are pie-in-the-sky as far as small firms and SMEs are concerned. There is no way you can undertake sophisticated research on a strictly limited budget and you are forced to rely, ultimately, on your personal intuition and judgement. Nevertheless, you can still undertake some useful, small-scale, low-cost 'research' and the fundamental principles of marketing research are the same no matter what the size of the business.

■ The information you need to gather

Good research is as much to do with the spirit of enquiry as with particular investigative techniques, which are bound to be imprecise anyway. All firms need to ask the same questions when conducting market research, including the following.

157

- What sorts of customers are likely to buy from the firm – business or personal, large or small, old or young, rich or poor?
- Where are customers located and how can they best be reached?
- What causes consumers to buy the firm's particular type of product?
- How extensive is the competition and what is its quality? How do competitors set their prices, advertise and generally market their products?
- How much are customers willing to pay for the firm's output?
- Is the market likely to expand, contract or alter in character, and how does it react to new products and/or changes in price?

Several conventional market research techniques can be adapted for use by small businesses or SMEs, particularly those outlined below.[4]

■ Market surveys

As the owner of a small firm or SME, you have the advantage that you come into direct personal contact with customers and, thus, can ask them for their views on your products, how they are presented, about desired quality levels, customer reactions to product prices, after-sales service required (and how much customers are prepared to pay for this) and so on.

■ Define your market

Avoid defining potential markets too broadly as this might cause you to ignore the need for different marketing methods in various market segments. For example, local customers might be best serviced by retail outlets and/or a direct delivery network, whereas national customers could require an expensive mail-order system.

You cannot afford to undertake much primary field research, so you must become adept at finding out whether or not anyone else has already investigated certain markets. It may be, for instance, that local population surveys have been conducted showing the number of people in the business' catchment area, their income per head and age and sex distribution. Trade journals (which you should read avidly) might survey particular markets, and local competitors may be quickly identified by looking in your *Yellow Pages*.

Multiplying the number of potential customers (identified according to age, income, occupation, social status and so on) in the firm's catchment area by target sales per customer gives the financial value of the maximum market size. Divide this by the number of competitors plus one and the figure you are left with can be used as the target market share for your next year of operation. Do not assume the firm's market share will exceed this because substantial periods might elapse before customers become aware of your business' revival.

■ Use of questionnaires

Valuable information can be obtained from simple questionnaires asking for customers' views on various aspects of your firm and its products. These can be handed to customers when they buy or enclosed with invoices or other mailed business documents.

Postal questionnaires are cheap to distribute, and people who respond normally do so quickly. However, response rates may be low, and replies are constrained by the wording of questions – respondents do not usually elaborate on their immediate responses. Keep your questions short, clear, simple, logical and capable of speedy (and cheap) clerical cross-tabulation of answers.

■ Telephone surveys

Some marketing research can be done by telephone. The method is cheap, convenient (no travelling is involved) and a wide geographical area can be covered. It is particularly suitable if you do not personally come into contact with customers. Problems will arise, however, if:

■ you find it difficult to sound pleasant over the telephone;
■ respondents are busy when the call is made and thus do not want to answer questions;
■ secretaries and/or switchboard operators rebuff your approaches.

■ Interviews with customers

Ask selected customers for views on your products and presentation. Most customers are willing to be interviewed, provided the exercise is short and simple. Also, the process will create in customers a sense of involvement with your firm.

Although face-to-face interviews can elicit answers to questions appearing on questionnaires or checklists, less structured approaches – whereby customers are encouraged to talk openly about the firm and its products – are also worth undertaking. In the latter case, open-ended rather than 'yes/no' questions should be asked, and you should not seek to direct the course of the interview.

SUMMARY

Marketing is more than just 'selling', although higher levels of profitable sales are obviously the ultimate aim of such activities. Simply providing a good product at a reasonable price is not sufficient to achieve the best possible sales.

You have to be an all-rounder where marketing is concerned. Evaluate market opportunities before you decide your selling strategies, relating your product's attributes to customer needs. Different aspects of marketing will need to be emphasised according to the particular circumstances of your firm.

Marketing activities must be integrated and consistent. For example, there is no point spending lots of money on one marketing activity (advertising, for instance) if you do not have support facilities (a distribution system, attractive packaging, point-of-sale literature and so on) to back it up.

There are five major steps involved in formulating a marketing strategy:

- **product positioning;**
- **market segmentation;**
- **choosing a price;**
- **selecting promotional methods;**
- **deciding when to introduce new products and when to withdraw old ones.**

The tactics associated with your marketing strategy should include policies for branding output, creating suitable business images and

for public relations as a whole.

Personal selling is an important marketing skill and you should constantly seek to improve your selling skills. Work on your sales techniques: experiment, improvise, and keep careful records of the effectiveness of various approaches to prospective customers.

✓ Checklist

- ☐ When did you last ask a customer what they thought of your output without revealing that you are the owner of the firm?

- ☐ List six reasons a consumer should buy your output rather than that of your leading competitor.

- ☐ Have you a system for identifying changes in consumers' needs?

- ☐ When did you last devise an attractive new display of your goods?

- ☐ Is your packaging sufficiently attractive?

- ☐ If you operate at the top end of the market, could you develop an economy version of your product, and vice versa?

- ☐ What brand images attach to your output?

- ☐ Have you consciously attempted to segment your markets?

- ☐ Can you describe the lifestyles of your last three customers?

- ☐ How frequently do you vary your advertising messages to make them attractive to various market segments?

- ☐ How many more units do you believe you could sell if you cut your prices by 10 per cent?

- ☐ Have you considered using a loss leader, and what would be the implications of loss leading for the total revenues of the firm?

- ☐ When did you last consider using the following forms of sales promotion for your output:
    - coupons;
    - free samples;
    - a competition;
    - free gifts?

- ☐ List five attractive new names for your firm.

☐ What are the average unit profitabilities of each of your products? To what extent are differences in unit profitabilities explained by price differences rather than differences in production cost?

☐ Does your leading competitor operate in a market that you have not entered, and, if so, how long would it take you to enter that market?

☐ Does your firm possess a distinctive logo? If so, how recently did you consider altering it in order to enhance its appeal?

☐ How do you think your last three customers recognised the 'corporate identity' of your firm?

☐ How many items obviously based on business' press releases appeared in last week's edition of your local giveaway newspaper?

☐ Do you feel self-conscious when selling face to face? If you do, why is this?

☐ How much did you know about the backgrounds of your last three customers prior to contacting them?

☐ Have you prepared checklists to help you develop a sales pitch?

☐ What is the ratio of enquiries to customer orders for your products?

☐ What caused your last three lost customers to withdraw their trade?

☐ How closely do you monitor market trends and how do you do this?

Advertising and sales promotions

1
2
3
4
5
6
7
8
9
10
11
12

INTRODUCTION

The importance of effective marketing for the growth and development of a small firm cannot be overemphasised. Advertising and sales promotions (special offers, discounts, coupon distributions, competitions and so on) are the cutting edges of marketing practice, and failure to take them seriously is one of the commonest causes of underperformance among small businesses. This chapter tells you how to draft advertisements and devise and organise inexpensive, but profitable, promotions. It explains the key elements of attractive display, and how to write your own sales literature.

ADVERTISING

Small businesses usually cannot afford television or radio advertising and, thus, rely primarily on local newspaper advertisements, entries in the *Yellow Pages* and direct mail leaflets distributed door to door. You can draft these yourself and need not employ expensive professional advisers. Every penny you spend on advertising should be made to work hard on your behalf, so great care is necessary in segmenting markets (see Chapter 7), targeting potential customers and selecting appropriate messages. This section presents a do-it-yourself guide to writing copy for advertisements. Proceed as follows.

- List the desired outcomes of your advertising activities. Messages that succeed in creating awareness of your business and its products might not be so good for inducing people to visit your premises or write to the firm. Other aims could be to generate enquiries, counteract competitors' advertisements, create list of names and addresses for direct mail and so on.
- List and briefly describe the selling points of your product – for example, low cost, high efficiency, easy to install, credit available, a new flavour, a special offer, an attractive package, that the product conserves energy, uses less space. Select from this list just two or three attributes that you consider especially important to customers and highlight the most attractive as your major selling

proposition. This should define why your version of the product is superior to any other available.

- Write a headline based on the major selling proposition, stating that, for example, the product works efficiently, is cheap, attractive or has some other desirable feature. The headline should be eye-catching, arouse interest, perhaps even be provocative in style. If you get stuck when trying to think up a suitable headline, look for inspiration to the hundreds of advertisement headlines you see around you every week in newspapers, magazines on direct mail advertisements and posters. Select a model and improvise on the chosen theme. Cannibalise various headlines until you have something you think fits.

- Devise an illustration to insert below, above or superimpose over the headline. This can be a photograph (possibly of the product in use or of a typical consumer) or a line-drawing commissioned from your printer. Its purposes are to reinforce the headline message and present the product attractively, so it must be visually appealing and large enough to impress.

- Draft 'body copy' for insertion in one, two or three columns immediately below the illustration (or headline if this itself follows the illustration). Stick to the following rules:
  - avoid technical and unintelligible jargon that consumers will not understand;
  - explain the headline, using short, simple sentences, usually with just one sentence per paragraph;
  - justify claimed advantages, mentioning extra selling points and, where appropriate, the costs and disadvantages of being without the product;
  - be brief and accurate, and make the points sound interesting. Inform readers of things they need to know. Again, you might look at existing press advertisements for other products to inspire and guide your thoughts.

- Position your business' name and logo prominently in a lower corner of the advertisement. Put supply details alongside your business name – that is, state how, when and where the customer can obtain or experience the product, say, by phoning a certain number, filling in a coupon, visiting your showroom or writing to the firm.

- End the advertisement with a 'tag line' (or 'exit line') running across all or part of the bottom of the advertisement. A tag line is a brief summary statement reinforcing the advertisement's basic theme or summing up the character of the product. Most press advertisements have tag lines. Look at magazine and newspaper advertisements for examples.

None of these rules is hard and fast, and you will observe many variations in the structures of advertisements that appear in magazines (the *Radio Times* and *TV Times* are good places to look) and in newspapers. In general, however, aim for a balanced appearance to the advertisement, with a single focal point – located halfway across the advertisement and, perhaps, one third the way down its length – to fix the reader's attention. A good advertisement:

- informs the reader;
- creates within them a desire to possess the product;
- makes it easy for the customer to convert this desire into action by directing the reader to behave in an appropriate way – by, for example, making a telephone call, filling in a form, visiting the firm and so on.

■ Code your advertisements

Each campaign should carry a code, enabling the easy identification of responses (use differing department references in the address you quote, slightly different response form designs and so on) and, hence, the effectiveness or otherwise of advertising expenditures. Be sure to relate the number of enquiries an advertisement elicits to the volume of orders eventually received. If many enquiries result from an advertisement, but hardly any actual sales, this indicates perhaps, that the advertisement overstated the objective worth of the product, causing disappointment among consumers who inspected the goods.

■ Outdoor advertising

Posters can be difficult to design, costly to print and poster sites are expensive to hire. Unless there are particular reasons for using posters (if you run a hotel, for example, you probably need a conspicuous poster near the local railway station or you might require additional point-of-sale advertising alongside retail outlets), you should think twice before committing yourself to this expense.

■ Mobile advertisements

More useful to the small business, perhaps, is an attractive display specifying your line of business and telephone number on the side and back panels of vehicles operated by the firm. Back panels face the drivers of the cars behind you and, thus, can usefully contain a lot of detail because the advertisement will be read carefully by following drivers in slow-moving traffic. However, adverts on side panels need to have large, bold letters for your firm's name and description of its business because onlookers will have only a brief glance at the vehicle as it passes. If a particular bus route passes through an area containing a high density of potential customers, then it may be worth while hiring an advertising space on an upper or lower deck interior side panel.

SALES PROMOTIONS

Every business needs a promotional strategy for its products. Begin with a statement of who you want your material to reach, and what you want consumers to do or feel as they receive the messages it conveys. Thus, for example, a competition or sweepstake can be used to create consumer awareness. Money off offers, free gifts or coupons, on the other hand,

Every business needs a promotional strategy for its products.

might be useful for encouraging customer loyalty. Depending on the nature of your business, you can devise special refunds, 'buy one, get one free' offers, cut price samples, cross-couponing and banded packaging (that is, a big price reduction on one item is available if another product is purchased at the same time) and so on.

Perhaps you haven't previously considered employing these devices, but just think of their potential advantages. They can be used to:

- reach entirely new markets;
- further penetrate existing markets;
- retain custom;
- expedite the launch of a new product;
- smooth out seasonal demand;
- stimulate repeat purchases;
- secure impulse purchases;
- shift slow-moving stock;

and generally draw attention to your firm and its products. Promotions need not be expensive and, because of their immediate impact, may provide precisely the shot in the arm your business requires. They may be adapted to attract specific target groups (particularly at the point of sale), and they enhance the brand images you have already created.

■ Which promotion?

Choice of a particular promotional technique should depend on your promotional objectives. Are you aiming primarily to stimulate impulse purchases, penetrate new markets or encourage loyalty to the product? Concentrate on the areas you are least good at. If consumer loyalty to your product is already strong, there is little point in devising a promotional strategy aimed at enhancing repeat purchases. Instead, you should be seeking to attract completely new customers in different market segments.

TYPES OF PROMOTION

The main types of sales promotion are:

- linked-product discounts or gifts;
- cash reductions – possibly by means of coupons;
- competitions – subject to certain legal requirements;
- free samples and gifts;
- self-liquidating premiums.

■ Linked-product offers

These may involve banded packs or cross-couponing. The idea is to persuade consumers to sample one product, having already purchased something else.

■ *Banded packaging*

Banded packaging means connecting the packages of two items with glue or tape (as happens when a toiletries manufacturer bands together soap and toothpaste packets, for example). The two items are then put on sale for a total price that is lower than they would cost if purchased individually. Essentially, you offer the consumer a sample of one of the items, but do not have to give it away.

Banding encourages impulse purchases and is extremely useful for shifting slow-moving stock. You need to ensure, of course, that outlets do not split banded packs and resell the items at higher prices.

Note that banded products do not have to be physical goods. Services can also be offered at a reduced rate when accompanied by others. Use your imagination to think up ways of applying the concept in your own business.

■ *Cross-couponing*

Cross-couponing is the practice of issuing a money off coupon for a product when a different product is purchased. It aims to encourage customer sampling of the coupon product and, thus, create entirely new consumer demand.

■ Cash reductions

Cash reductions occur directly via price cuts marked on flashpacks (that is, specially printed packages that display the price cut or increased quality prominently) or indirectly via cash refunds to customers who furnish proof of purchase after buying the goods. The latter method encourages repeat purchases and, importantly, the customers who send in proofs of purchase provide you with names and addresses for subsequent use in future direct mail activities. Refunds may be paid in the form of a money off voucher for the customer's next purchase – thus further increasing their loyalty to your firm – rather than in cash or by postal order.

■ Redemption rates

The problem with this type of promotion lies primarily in forecasting the redemption rate. Goods that are frequently purchased normally involve higher redemption rates because the requisite number of proofs of purchase (package tops, for example) is easier to obtain and this increases the total cost of the promotion. The more attractive the offer, the higher the redemption rate, yet the greater the number of redemptions the more expensive the offer becomes. (Vouchers rather than straight cash refunds are, in fact, more economical because not all vouchers issued to customers will actually be traded in.)

It is essential, therefore, that you assess the likely redemption rate by conducting a small-scale test of the offer's appeal prior to launching the full promotion. Note that refunds may be graduated to accommodate varying levels of consumer loyalty. For example, a 10 pence voucher might be offered in exchange for 10 proofs of purchase, whereas £1 could be given for 20. The proofs of purchase need to be identifiably related to the items on special offer, not to existing retail or consumer stocks.

■ Coupons

Money off coupons may be printed on a product's package, enclosed with the item or incorporated into newspaper advertisements or leaflets distributed door to door. They serve many purposes, including market penetration, encouragement of repeat purchases, sampling by new customers, higher levels of consumption, impulse purchases and so on. Coupons are most appropriate for small-value items sold by one business to another, though even here some equivalents of couponing may occur.

■ Coupon redemptions

Not all the coupons issued will be used, so you need to estimate the redemption rate. This will depend primarily on the value of the coupon, its aesthetic appeal and the extent of its distribution. Numerous secondary influences exist, such as the method of delivery, redemption period, frequency of purchase in shops and so on, and you will certainly need a trial run. As a rule of thumb allow for 2 or 3 per cent redemption from coupons in newspaper advertisements, 10 per cent from leaflets distributed door to door and 30 per cent from mail shots and coupons contained in or on packaging.

Problems with coupons

There is certainly no shortage of coupons currently circulating that you can base the design of your own coupon on – they arrive through the letterbox daily, and note how readily you can weave an advertising message into one. However, if you sell through retailers, they will demand compensation for handling the coupons, and they might redeem your coupon against any item purchased by the coupon holder.

Regular issuing of coupons creates further problems as customers may become accustomed to the effectively lower sale price of the product and thus resent subsequent withdrawal of the coupon offer. Moreover, regular users – who would buy the product anyway at the usual price – also benefit, thus reducing your aggregate returns.

Distribution

Target the distribution of your coupons at carefully selected consumer groups (blanket distributions are expensive to administer and potentially wasteful) and select the media for carrying the coupons with the target consumer groups in mind. Choose 'on pack' coupons if you wish to stimulate brand loyalty and repeat purchases, but recognise that redemption rates (and, hence, the cost to your business) will be higher via this medium. Use leaflets containing coupons if you wish to make direct consumer appeals. Also, always make sure you can identify the sales resulting from a particular channel. As a small business operating on a strictly limited budget, consider the feasibility of producing (with a word processor and photocopier) your own coupon promotion material and distributing it personally door to door. This avoids the need for costly newspaper advertisements (which may not be read by target consumer groups) and ensures that the offer goes directly into the potential customer's home. You may be able to do the distribution in your spare time, and might even get the family to help.

■ Competitions

Competitions are enormously popular among consumers, but there are substantial legal restrictions on the circumstances in which a competition can take place. Under the UK Gaming Acts, 1960 and 1968, any competition involving a purchase as the means of entry must include some element of skill. A 'luck of the draw' competition is illegal unless no product purchase is required, yet the absence of a proof of purchase makes the promotion essentially useless from the business' point of view. To overcome this difficulty, you must incorporate into the competition some means whereby the entrant exercises judgement. For example, you could ask them to state, in not more than a dozen words, why they prefer your product or to answer some easy questions. The restriction does not apply to trade (non-retail consumer) competitions, although, obviously, trade buyers are unlikely to purchase goods just to enter a competition.

■ *Uses of competitions*

A competition might be used to create consumer awareness of a product, penetrate a new market, stimulate impulse buying and encourage repeat purchase as well. An important advantage is that you know in advance how much the promotion will cost (there is no redemption rate to be estimated, no cash refunds or free gift problems) and administration need not be expensive. News of the competition can be incorporated into your normal advertising literature and/or be disseminated via retail outlets. The effect of a competition on sales will depend on the:

- attractiveness of the prize offered;
- level of difficulty of questions asked;
- number of proofs of purchase needed to enter;
- period for which the competition is open;
- how extensively the competition is advertised.

■ Free gifts

Impulse purchasing can sometimes be stimulated by attaching a small free gift to a prominent part of the outside of a package. The cost of the free gift reduces the mark-up on the item, but sales will increase and administrative costs are minimal. 'Mail ins' require consumers to send proofs of purchase through the post in order to claim the gift. When the gift is dispatched it is, of course, accompanied by further promotional literature.

■ *Problems with free gifts*

The problem is the cost of the giveaway item. Thus, many firms recoup some of their expenditure by offering items at greatly reduced prices rather than giving them away free.

Mail ins do generate their own mailing lists for subsequent use in further direct mail activities, and consumer loyalty increases. However, response rates must be estimated (you are legally obliged to supply the offered item or something of equivalent value to anyone providing the requisite number of proofs of purchase) and many people who claim the gift may have bought the product in any case. As a rule of thumb, think in terms of one purchaser in a hundred taking up the offer. Items distributed as free gifts should be:

- appealing;
- easily described or illustrated in promotional literature;
- convenient to deliver;
- safe to use;
- in keeping with the product's image – so high-quality products require high-quality promotions to reinforce their attraction.

As a small business, you cannot afford to store large quantities of the gift in anticipation of a high take-up rate, so choose something you can obtain easily 'off the peg' from several sources. Note that under section 46 [1](f) of the Consumer Protection Act 1987, any item given away (or offered as a prize in a raffle or competition) must be safe, and that the firm is liable to pay unlimited compensation to those injured if an item turns out to be defective.

■ Self-liquidating offers

An important advantage of 'self-liquidating' offers (that is, those requiring a contribution from customers) is that the degree of self-liquidation can be varied. Thus, you might offer the extra item completely free if the customer mails in, say, 10 proofs of purchase, or for £3 plus 5 proofs, or £6 plus 3 proofs. This extends the appeal of the offer from regular users (who will opt for ten purchases and no cash payment) to the occasional user who is encouraged to buy the product just three times. Note, moreover, that many people purchase specially marked packs intending to send off the money and proofs of purchase, but never actually do so, thus reducing your costs.

Careful costing is essential to the success of this type of offer. First, you must do an experimental trial run to estimate the extent of demand for the special packages, then you obtain the purchase costs of various batch sizes of the item to be offered, assess the costs of advertising the offer and, finally, compute your administration, handling and postage expenses. A gross miscalculation here can ruin your business, so check everything carefully.

■ Support for local charities

Your public image might be considerably enhanced if you visibly support a local charity, evidenced perhaps by your advertising in its publications, shop window or other media. You could, for example, offer to donate money in proportion to the volume of your trade during a pre-specified period (say, by paying so

Supporting a charity demonstrates your commitment to the local community and that your business is here to stay.

much to the charity for each proof of purchase sent to you in a particular month) up to a maximum amount. Supporting a charity demonstrates your commitment to the local community and that your business is here to stay. Charity promotions, moreover, can be tailor-made to support other advertising activities and to reinforce the 'corporate image' your firm projects as your business name is widely circulated and is perceived in a favourable light.

SALES PROMOTIONS VERSUS DISCOUNTS

An advantage of sales promotions generally is that they attract new business without the need to offer easy credit or highly expensive discounts for prompt settlement of accounts. Debt collecting is expensive, but special promotions typically give customers incentives that are independent of the system for credit control. Even a device as simple as offering free delivery on large cash orders can be cheaper than the administrative and other costs of extended credit. True, the administration of sales promotions incurs costs (printing or photocopying the literature, postage, refund costs, advertising the offer), but at least they increase sales – easy credit terms usually do not!

> *An advantage of sales promotions generally is that they attract new business without the need to offer easy credit or highly expensive discounts for prompt settlement of accounts.*

■ Discounts as a means of sales promotion

Certain discounts, however, have promotional value, for example:

- quantity discounts – if taken up, these will enable you to economise on your holdings of finished goods stocks, and the fact that customers are induced to buy in greater numbers encourages them to actively promote the sale of your product;
- forward buying discounts – goods are ordered today under a contractually binding agreement for delivery on specified future dates;
- free delivery or free extra goods on certain sizes of order – for example, buy six cases, get one free;
- straight cash bonuses on quantities sold through particular outlets;
- *ad hoc* payments to new stockists and payments to existing outlets that introduce new stockists to you.

The discounts you offer should not mislead customers into believing that the price quoted is lower than it actually is. Otherwise you could commit an offence under the Consumer Protection Act 1987 (see Chapter 9). If in doubt, check with your local trading standards office.

TRADE DEALS

People in business are not prepared to do things for free – they require incentives to induce them to behave in particular ways. To the extent that you have to rely on other firms to sell your output, you need to offer them financial inducements to promote your goods. Trade deals and bonuses are pre-planned payments to retailers or distributors for extra services or favours.

Retailers, in particular, are concerned with the 'shelf life' of your product as they dislike having money tied up for long periods in slow-moving stock. Perhaps, therefore, you can devise an incentive that compensates the retailer in part for carrying a slow-moving item and thus encourages larger orders. In return for the payment (and, hence, a higher profit margin on selling the product) the retailer should be asked to display your goods prominently and guide customers towards them when customers seem indifferent as to which brand to select. In consequence:

- your product sells faster;
- the retailer obtains a higher unit margin on a higher volume of sales;
- your competitors' products are crowded out from key display positions.

Try to link trade deals with forthcoming sales promotions (coupon or money off offers, for example) that make your product even more attractive to stock. Note, however, that trade deals are not suitable for goods that are well established and already occupy prominent display positions in retail outlets.

Offering a trade deal is a bit of a gamble. Retailers and distributors might increase current purchases in order to obtain the bonus, but, in effect, may simply bring forward the timing of their orders, so aggregate purchases might not be affected in the longer run. Nevertheless, your business does receive an injection of short-term funds as a result and if you tie the bonus to increased retail sales and/or enhanced display, then the additional goods taken will hopefully be sold quickly and thus lead to further orders for your firm.

SALES PROMOTIONS LAW

Certain ethical standards must be maintained in the implementation of sales promotions, which should be honest and legal, with expiry dates and other limitations on the offer clearly printed on the outside of the pack. (See the Advertising Standards Authority's *British Code of Practice on Sales Promotions* for further details.) Offers that require proof of purchase prior to your paying out should involve proofs that are unique to the product under offer, which are easily removed from the package and easy to send through the post. Application forms for redemption should be legible and provide sufficient space for the customer's name and address.

Free gifts can only be described as 'free' if there is no charge for handling, packaging or administration. If postage is required, this fact should be stated on the offer. It is illegal to state that an offered item is worth more than its actual value, and you cannot incorporate the logo of the firm that makes the item into your promotional literature without the manufacturer's permission.

Medicinal products, especially those available to the public without prescription, are subject to special legal control. Accordingly, the Medicines (Labelling) Amendment Act 1977 requires that all containers and packages of such products carry the words 'Keep out of reach of children' or other words of similar meaning. Free, random distribution of samples of medicine to the general public is illegal under the Medicines Act 1968.

Any promotion that might be construed as incorporating a lottery – that is, a free draw where success depends entirely on chance – creates special difficulties. The Lotteries and Amusements Act 1976 (and subsequent regulations issued under the Act) states that a lottery is legal only if:

- no proof of purchase is involved;
- it is not passed off as a competition;
- all entries have an equal probability of success;
- prizes are clearly defined.

Thus, a money off coupon distributed door to door that is also used as a draw ticket is quite legal, provided the coupon clearly states that entry to the draw is possible without buying the product. Similar considerations apply to sweepstakes. In either case, the price of each ticket must be the same, and tickets must state:

- the name and address of the promoters;
- the date of the draw and the prizes available;
- that prizes will only be delivered to purchasers of winning tickets.

DISPLAY AND MERCHANDISING

If you rely on retailers selling your output, encourage some of them – perhaps via financial inducements – to have special displays of your product(s) away from normal shelf positions or otherwise to draw special attention to the product.

The display should surround the goods with promotional materials – a poster, leaflets, special offer coupons, invitations to participate in a competition and so on – that attract consumer interest and encourage them to buy.

■ Dump displays

A dump display might be appropriate for your needs. This consists of a big stack of units of your product strategically piled up in the middle of an aisle in such a way that consumers cannot avoid confronting the display. Similarly, an appealing layout of the product just where customers enter or leave the outlet may increase sales. These interrupt the normal 'traffic flow' of customers within a shop and, thus, lead to a higher level of impulse purchases. The problem is one of convincing the retailer that:

- you both have a common interest in shifting the product quickly;
- your suggestions about how best to display the product will lead to an increase in sales.

■ Do-it-yourself merchandising

Study the nature of trade in the catchment area of the retail outlet concerned and ask yourself what sorts of display are most likely to impress the customer types who frequent that establishment. Now examine the shop's layout, its customer traffic flow, position of pillars and doorways, and the current locations of major product categories.

Next, identify the best positions for displaying your product. Normally the most attractive positions are the natural high-traffic areas around:

- the perimeter of the outlet – customers tend to keep to the outer edges of gondola layouts;
- entry doors – which are usually placed to the side of the shop window, so that at least half of all customers must pass the entire window display before entering;
- shelves containing high-demand items – where the customer flow automatically slows down and, hence, where impulse purchases are more likely;
- checkouts – which are an obvious source of customer traffic congestion.

Explain to the retailer that a special display of your product, especially a dump display, will give atmosphere to the shop, enhance its general appearance and increase consumer spending to your mutual benefit. Importantly, special displays between gondolas can be used to control traffic flow and, thus, encourage customers to shop in certain sections they might otherwise overlook. Also, the existence of an in-store display distinguishes the retail outlet from its competitors and so helps create a progressive and competitive image for the firm.

DIRECT MAIL

Obviously face-to-face contact with customers is desirable because it allows instant communication with and feedback from them. You can listen to people, ask them questions and really get to know what makes them tick. The problem is that personal selling absorbs large amounts of time and so is very expensive. Also, there are travel and accommodation costs, and there is a physical limit to the number of customers who can be seen in this way.

For many small businesses, therefore, direct mail is a more attractive and cost-effective proposition. Opportunities for contacting customers via this medium abound. You can write to people about special offers, new products, after-sales service, price cuts, the latest fashions or simply to say thank you for buying from the firm.

Direct mail encompasses both mail order selling and the distribution of advertising and other promotional literature to target consumer segments by post. All you need to operate a direct mail system are a cheap word processor, paper, a photocopying facility and a relevant, accurate and up-to-date list of names and addresses.

Mailing lists can be obtained in several ways.

■ You can compile a list of the names and addresses of customers who have replied to your mail order advertisements in newspapers or to leaflets distributed door to door.

■ You can search appropriate sections in the *Yellow Pages* and other business directories (such as national directories of the Chamber of Commerce) available in your local library or perhaps simply by inspecting the electoral roll.

■ You can use the services of mailing list brokers who sell lists of names and address to other firms. All the subjects on a particular list will belong to a group of consumers who exhibit certain characteristics, such as being owners of expensive cars, interested in wildlife, members of various types of organisations, mortgagees, members of certain ethnic and religious groups or whatever. A list broker might, for example, sell you a list of owners of a certain type of motor car, from a particular ethnic group or religion, living in a certain town, who spend more than a certain amount per month on a particular product. List brokers themselves purchase names and addresses from other organisations (the Automobile Association, financial institutions, churches, sporting and cultural bodies, and so on) that are prepared to disclose their members' whereabouts. Then the list broker cross-tabulates names and addresses according to your needs. Brokers will also administer the campaign (including the design of promotional literature) for an additional fee. The Royal Mail publishes a range of pamphlets concerning these matters, including details of where to go to rent or purchase lists.

■ Mail order

Mail order business arises from customers returning order forms enclosed with direct mail or completing order forms included in newspaper advertisements or leaflets. This type of selling is ideal for servicing customer groups that are unable to purchase your product via normal retail outlets, say, because of their working hours, lifestyles or geographical location. To reach these consumer groups, you may need to organise a targeted mail drop. If it is done properly, this could evoke a substantial response – even a 1 per cent response can be cost-effective. Alternatively, you could advertise in particular local newspapers or special interest magazines.

A problem with press advertising of mail order items (apart from typically low response rates) is that if you include a money off coupon, or a name and address panel for the reader to complete or anything else that needs cutting out (hence disfiguring the printed page), then you will usually achieve a higher response if you position the advertisement at the bottom right-hand corner of the page, where the response form is easier to remove. Unfortunately, some newspapers and magazines charge extra for this location. Full details of these (and other) charges are printed monthly in the *BRAD* press guide (which stands for *British Rate and Data*). It covers all UK publications that carry advertisements and is available in most public libraries.

Unique selling points

Mail order customers are typically attracted to goods that are unique or unusual in some way, so direct your advertising messages at the unique selling points of your products – their special features, ease of use, charm, good looks, low price or whatever. A 'no quibble' money back guarantee on mail order goods (including a refund of the return postage) is a useful selling point, which should be prominently displayed in advertising messages. Note that customers are rarely willing to send high-value cheques for goods they have not inspected. Thus, low-priced items are more appropriate for mail order trade. Unfortunately, this means that postage, packing, transit breakages, handling and administration costs necessarily account for a relatively large part of the final sale price of the product. Hence, you may be compelled to accept lower profit margins on the output you sell by mail.

■ Office of Fair Trading (OFT) rules

Because mail order customers are expected to part with their money before seeing goods, the OFT specifies precise guidelines for mail-order operations. In response to these, several trade associations have introduced 'mail order protection schemes'. The most important of these are operated by the:

- Newspaper Publishers Association (NPA) – covering the national press;
- Newspaper Society (NS) – representing local newspapers;
- Periodical Publishers Association (PPA) – for magazines;
- Independent Broadcasting Authority (IBA).

Such schemes aim to protect mail order customers and compensate those who lose money by buying things mail order. A central fund is created into which all member organisations contribute and from which claims are paid. Each member then imposes a small levy on every mail order firm advertising in its publications.

■ The NPA scheme

National newspapers belong to the NPA scheme, and you must subscribe to this before any national newspaper will accept your mail order advertisement. You apply initially to the paper in which you wish to advertise, pay the appropriate fee (which depends on the total annual value of the advertisements you place with NPA members) and must provide evidence that your business is financially sound – that is, it is well established (or has substantial assets if it is new), is trading profitably and employs reliable and experienced staff.

The NPA then takes up credit references and might send a representative to inspect your premises. If the NPA is not fully satisfied, it may insist that you offer a substantial bank guarantee or possess appropriate insurance cover before entering the scheme. Other mail order protection (MOP) systems operate in a similar fashion.

Customers who lose money as a result of the bankruptcy, company liquidation or fraud of an advertiser belonging to a MOP scheme are entitled to a full refund, with the following exceptions, which cannot be covered by MOP:

- any kind of foodstuff;
- contraceptives or other sexually related items;
- products that appeal to fear or superstition, such as lucky charms or horoscopes.

Note that you need to join a MOP scheme only if customers are required to pay prior to receiving the goods. If your advertisement merely invites customers to send for a catalogue or low-cost brochure or visit your premises or order returnable goods on approval, then you do not have to become a member. Also, each MOP system has its own special exemptions (see Note 1 at the end of this chapter).

■ Advantages of direct mail

Direct mail has several advantages:

- unlike most advertising, it may be carefully targeted at particular groups;
- it can be designed to carry a personal appeal;
- no sales people are necessary;
- responses are quickly, accurately and easily assessed;
- you can experiment with different types of mail drop literature, send it to differing consumer categories and observe the response, and you can vary the geographical areas covered;
- much direct mail work you can do yourself, without recourse to newspaper advertisements, expensive agents, publicity gimmicks and so on.

The cost per customer contact is substantial, but cost-effective – provided you target your market segments with care. Ensure that mail drops are easy to reply to and 'code' the responses (say, by using differing PO box numbers, different 'departments' in the reply address, or incorporating visible differences in the response forms) in order to measure consumer reactions to various campaigns.

■ Sales literature

The material sent to potential customers via direct mail might comprise an existing advertisement reproduced on a leaflet, plus an accompanying letter. Alternatively, you could devise a self-contained 'one-piece mailer' consisting of promotional messages, body copy and order form, all incorporated into a single document. Whichever way you do it, the basic principles are the same. You must:

- firmly establish the identity of the firm and the nature of its business;
- explain the claims made in your advertisement and/or document headline;
- provide information – such as what the product does, how it works, why it should be purchased – and generally reinforce other promotional messages.

When drafting the document, ask yourself repeatedly why anyone should want to buy your output and not that of competing firms. What are the product's exclusive qualities? What advantages does it offer over other brands? What attributes and benefits does it possess? The end part of the document should stimulate the reader to take positive steps to acquire the product. Reiterate the major selling proposition and state – precisely and straightforwardly – how the item may be ordered and give details of any discount or credit terms that apply. Use short and simple sentences, lots of headings and paragraphs that consist of just one or two sentences.

Most recipients of mail drop do in fact open the envelopes containing the sales literature, but only spend a few seconds inspecting the contents. Immediate visual impact is thus critically important to a campaign's success.

There are certain general rules to follow when devising a sales letter.

- Avoid technical jargon.
- Begin a sales letter with the name of the customer and not just 'Dear sir or madam'.
- Try not to irritate the reader by repeating points excessively.

- Use good-quality paper and envelopes.
- Personalise the literature. You can use the mail merge facility on a word processor to do this.
- Try to make your direct mail different to that of your competitors.
- Be brief and stick to the point of the exercise. Do not include superfluous material – instead, concentrate on dramatising the basic message contained in the literature.
- Do not offer special prices or terms you are not able or willing to provide.

If you experience a mental block while trying to think up appealing messages, seek inspiration from the numerous specimens of direct mail literature that come through your letterbox every week. Much of this will have been professionally, and expensively, produced by large organisations. Base your own material on the best bits of these examples – some are bound to contain approaches relevant to your needs. Cannibalise, reword, restructure and rework this material until you come up with something appropriate to your requirements (though be careful not to infringe copyright by directly lifting words and phrases from a single source).

Note that grossly inaccurate sales literature violates UK consumer protection legislation (see Chapter 9). If you are unsure of the precision of your descriptions, then qualify them with words such as 'approximately', 'probably', 'generally' and so on.

KEEPING CUSTOMERS FOR LIFE

Businesses that survive are those with loyal customers. Remember that it can cost anything up to six times more to get a new customer than to keep an existing one! Just think of all the benefits of obtaining fresh orders from your present customers. You don't have to spend as much money on advertising because your present clientèle will already be familiar with your products, and they will be less likely to worry about the price as they know they will be satisfied with their purchases. Also, it becomes more difficult for your competitors to gain market share. Regular customers tend to order more frequently and place larger orders, so cost less to service (in many firms about 20 per cent of customers account for 80 per cent of their total sales). Moreover they are likely to give your name to completely new customers at no extra cost whatsoever to yourself.

It follows that you need to build up good long-term relations with your customers. This is sometimes called 'relationship marketing', and is increasingly recognised as a vital ingredient of business success. To succeed at relationship marketing, it is essential that you develop the right attitude. This means that you need to genuinely care for your customers' best interests, want to provide the highest quality goods and services possible, be responsive to your customers' suggestions and be open and fair at all times. You have to see your customer as a partner in the business, not just somebody to whom you make a one-off sale.

To retain customers, you need to maintain contact with them. Customers want information from the businesses they deal with. Communicate with your customers as individuals – talk to them and encourage them to talk back. Here are some practical steps you can take to improve your long-term relationships with customers:

- always attempt to see things from the customer's point of view – this will help you to become involved with your customers' problems and understand their concerns;
- put customers first – do not regard customer care as a separate function, but, rather, look on it as an integral and inseperable part of everything your business does;
- provide customers with as much news as you can about your firm and its activities, irrespective of whether or not you expect to win a sale;
- devise and implement a system for dealing with customer complaints, as outlined below.

■ Customer complaints

Listening to customers' complaints can be an extremely valuable means of finding out about the performance of your firm and how it is regarded by outsiders. It seems, moreover, that the satisfactory handling of complaints can actually create business. Surveys of complaints from customers have revealed that more than 80 per cent of disgruntled customers who make a complaint and whose grievance is resolved quickly will continue to buy from the offending firm. Indeed, it is likely that a customer will be more highly motivated to make a purchase from you immediately following the successful resolution of a complaint than at any other time.

Other benefits to having sound complaints procedures are that:

- you gain a reputation for being a 'caring' business;
- customers are, in effect, providing you with free market research;
- 'hidden' problems that you might not have been aware of are uncovered;
- customers are given the opportunity to tell you about their grievances rather than anyone else;
- needs for staff training and product development may be identified;
- you develop your interpersonal skills;
- customer retention rates increase, leading to higher profitability.

Here are some 'do's and don'ts' for dealing with complaints.

Do:
- deal with the complaint quickly;
- apologise and say you want to make amends;
- explain how you are trying to overcome the problem;
- make the customer feel that you are doing everything you possibly can;
- keep detailed records of complaints and actions taken;
- tell the aggrieved customer what to do if they are still not satisfied;
- look for trends in the natures of complaints registered.

Don't:
- send the complainant a standard preprinted form;
- have the complaint processed by someone not conversant with all the facts;
- say you will get back to the customer and then fail to do so;
- forget to address and sign the letter personally;
- ignore underlying problems;
- fail to address your business' weaknesses.

■ Building a customer database

You don't need to be a computer genius to set up a customer database, and it doesn't have to cost much money. Indeed, you can even create a database manually using a card index system, although clearly the employment of a PC saves an enormous amount of time.

Start with a listing of the names, addresses, telephone numbers and so on of all existing customers, together with any other information you have about them – their lines of activity, for business customers, or sex and so on for individual customers. Then build up a profile of each customer in relation to such matters as:

- specific products purchased;
- frequency of each customer's purchases;
- enquiries and complaints received;
- how much money was spent on each order and how and when the firm or person paid the bill;
- the date of the last order (so that you can invite a fresh purchase at just the right time);
- responsiveness to mail shots or special promotions;
- how orders were placed (letter, telephone, personal visit or whatever);
- any special costs incurred when servicing particular customers.

The aim is to construct a complete history of your relationship with each customer so that you can contact them on a personal basis and offer them products and service levels that are precisely suited to their individual needs. Crucially, you will be able to break your customers down into categories, such as high spenders, low spenders, first-time buyers, frequent and infrequent purchasers and so on. This can be vitally important when deciding which type of approach to adopt when seeking fresh sales.

SUMMARY

Effective advertising and sales promotions are essential to the long-term survival of the small firm. You need not spend a fortune on these activities as much of the creative and administrative work attached to them you can do yourself.

Begin with a statement of the purposes of your promotional strategy, listing the specific outcomes you wish to achieve and by when. Then, describe all the selling points attached to your output. You need to be able to define precisely how and why your product is superior to those of your competitors.

People today are immersed in advertising messages and symbols and so, as a matter of course, they expect a business to present itself attractively. If you do not bother with advertising and promotion, consumers might think your output is defective in some way.

Seek inspiration from the advertisements and promotional methods of your competitors and other firms. Select an appropriate model and improvise on the chosen theme. Be on the lookout for illustrations that could be used to support advertising copy and note carefully any attractive logos belonging to businesses similar to your own.

Consider the applicability and feasibility of using each of the following types of sales promotion:

- a competition;
- a 'buy one, get one free' offer;
- packaging your product in a money off flashpack;
- a coupon offer;
- sponsorship of a local charity linked to levels of sales achieved;
- free samples or gifts.

Use promotions to improve sales performance in the areas in which you are weakest. Above all, be innovative in your general approach – experiment, devise new schemes, constantly modify your promotions (and advertisements) to make them more appealing to target consumer groups.

If your output is sold via retailers, visit their outlets and talk to the owners about how best to display your goods. Select the best display positions in each store and suggest that your products be located there. A small cash inducement to the retailer may be worth while if the very best display positions are secured.

Direct mail is increasingly important for marketing the output of small businesses. You can write your own direct mail sales literature according to certain predetermined and straightforward rules. There is no shortage of examples of direct mail literature distributed by other firms that you can base your own efforts on.

✓ Checklist

- ☐ Of the last £1000 you spent on advertising, how much of it can you be sure contributed significantly to achieving a higher level of sales?

- ☐ Do you draft your own advertising copy? If not, why not?

- ☐ What are the major selling points of your output (list at least ten of these), and what are the minor selling points?

- ☐ Why is your product superior to that of your competitors?

- ☐ When did you last revise your firm's logo?

- ☐ Are your business name, telephone number and line of work prominently displayed on the side and back panels of vehicles belonging to the firm?

- ☐ Which form of sales promotion is most likely to shift your slow-moving finished goods stock?

- ☐ Does each of your advertisements carry a tag line? If not, think up at least four such lines that you could use for this purpose.

- ☐ Do you code your advertisements in order to assess the responses from various campaigns?

- ☐ How many different ways of promoting your product have you tried during the last 12 months?

Note

1. For example, the NPA allows certain services, such as membership of a club or the sale of magazine subscriptions, to proceed without its approval. Also, any mail order advertisement may be placed in a national paper's 'classified' section regardless of NPA considerations.

Keeping within the law

1
2
3
4
5
6
7
8
9
10
11
12

INTRODUCTION

Previous chapters have cited various legal constraints on small business and SMEs, and there are indeed many legal considerations that need to be taken into account.

Small businesses and SMEs need to be particularly vigilant in relation to consumer protection (including consumer credit regulations), employee rights and health and safety at work. Chapter 6 has dealt with employment and safety, so this chapter focuses on consumer protection law, ignorance of which has caused many small firms and SMEs to fail.

DEFECTIVE PRODUCTS

Different countries adopt different approaches to the question of who is liable for damages caused by defective products. Some countries insist that the producer is liable, no matter what the circumstances. Others make suppliers liable only if the injured party can prove negligence on the supplier's part. Prior to 1987, the latter situation applied in the UK.

This contravened a 1985 EU directive on the subject, so, in order to bring UK practice into line with minimum EU requirements, the UK Parliament enacted the Consumer Protection Act 1987. The Act abandoned the need for plaintiffs to prove the supplier's negligence when pursuing defective product claims. However, it does not go so far as to render suppliers absolutely responsible for defects in their products. Instead, a supplier is generally liable, but not if they can demonstrate that the 'state of scientific and technical knowledge' at the time the product went into circulation was not such that a supplier could be reasonably expected to have known about the defect the product contains.

Under the Act, a 'producer' is not only the manufacturer of a finished article or its raw materials (or the extractor of raw materials) or the manufacturer of component parts, but may also include any firm or person who imports, processes, distributes or otherwise supplies (such as by hiring or lending) the product.

A 'product' is defined as any goods (including electricity) or part of another goods or raw material. Producers are liable for their products, as is any person or firm putting a name, trademark or distinguishing mark (such as a business logo) on the product. The victim of a defective product must ask the person or firm that supplied it to identify its producer and, if the supplier is unable to do this (that is, if the last known supplier cannot 'pass back' liability for the defect), then the last supplier is fully liable. If more than one producer is involved, then all are equally liable and if some are insolvent, then the remainder are responsible for meeting the entire claim. Customer complaints must be registered within three years of the purchase or within one year of the customer discovering the fault within this three-year period.

In deciding whether or not a product is 'defective', a court will examine:

- what it might reasonably be expected to do;
- how the product is marketed – that is, what the supplier claims it will do (described in the Act as the product's 'get-up');
- any operating instructions, printed warnings and related literature accompanying the product.

■ Defences

Actions are not possible unless the damage allegedly caused exceeds £275. Confronted with a claim, you may assert that:

- you did not supply the goods;
- someone else produced it and is therefore liable – although if you cannot pass back liability (either because you are, in fact, the producer or the actual producer has disappeared or is insolvent) then you are fully responsible for the damage caused (unless you are a 'retailer' – see below);

> *Liability cannot be avoided by using exclusion clauses in sale agreements or posting notices around the point of sale denying responsibility.*

- the goods are not defective;

- the state of technical knowledge at the moment of supply could not reasonably lead you to suspect that the goods were defective;
- defects arose not within your product, but as a result of the way someone else made up or designed the final product into which it was incorporated.

Note, however, that liability cannot be avoided by using exclusion clauses in sale agreements or posting notices around the point of sale denying responsibility. Moreover, you must show that you were 'duly diligent' and took all reasonable steps to try to avoid committing an offence.

■ Consumer safety

The Act makes it illegal not only to supply unsafe goods, but also to:

- possess them – for example, by holding them in stock;
- provide inadequate instructions for their use, thereby causing accidents;
- fail to provide proper warnings of dangerous aspects of the goods;
- fail to apply all reasonable measures (having regard to cost and the likelihood of improvement) for improving the safety of goods.

Retailers have a special protection under the Act. They are not liable for the defective goods they sell, provided:

- they did not know the goods were unsafe;
- that such ignorance was reasonable in the particular circumstances.

It is interesting to note that tobacco is explicitly excluded from the Act. Cigarettes, therefore, are not a 'defective product', despite the deaths and illness they cause.

MISLEADING PRICE INDICATIONS

The Act states that it is a criminal offence (punishable by fine) to mislead consumers about product prices. A price indication is misleading if:

- the actual price is higher than that shown;
- the low price indicated depends on facts or circumstances not revealed to the customer;
- additional charges are not disclosed;
- the supplier makes out that the price will shortly be increased when this is not the case – for example, 'buy now to beat next month's price rise' when no such price increase is scheduled to occur.

Misleading price indications are unlawful in advertisements, catalogues, circulars and price lists as well as at the point of sale. The Act applies to services (including credit and banking services) as well as physical goods.

TRADE DESCRIPTIONS

The Act strengthens and updates some of the provisions of the Trade Descriptions Act 1968 (the 1972 update to this is replaced in its entirety), which established the general principle that it is illegal to advertise goods in such a way as to give incorrect, misleading or false information about them. In passing the Trade Descriptions Act, Parliament sought to prevent sellers from:

- publishing advertisements that contain false information about their merchandise;
- stating such information orally or in writing;
- displaying signs about their merchandise that might give a false impression.

Misleading statements might relate to the physical characteristics of a product – such as its size, weight, colour and so on – or its suitability for its intended purpose or to any other relevant characteristic. Goods may be 'described' via a label, a statement on packaging, statements in documents (guarantees, for example) relating to the goods or signs on, above, alongside or near the goods.

Sellers can avoid liability if they prove that a false description was given due to a genuine mistake or by accident, provided all reasonable precautions against mistakes and accidents had been taken.

THE SALE AND SUPPLY OF GOODS ACT 1994

This amended previous legislation by requiring that goods sold be of a 'satisfactory' quality – that is, that they meet the standard a reasonable person would regard as satisfactory, taking into consideration the way the goods were described, price and all other relevant circumstances. 'Quality' includes the state and condition of the goods, their 'fitness for purpose', appearance and finish, freedom from minor defects, safety and durability. Any defects must be clearly brought to the buyer's attention before the contract is made. There is no obligation on the buyers to examine the goods prior to purchase. Suppliers must deliver (or make available for collection) goods that correspond to the way in which they have been described or to a sample previously inspected.

Buyers can claim compensation if goods are not delivered and have the right to reject them on delivery if they do not correspond with the agreed details of the transaction. Customers are entitled to full compensation if goods prove to be defective or unfit for their purpose.

Under the legislation, a supplying firm is not lawfully able to impose a condition on a sale, saying that the supplier does not accept responsibility for their quality, suitability or delivery. Such a statement is of no effect and the buyer is still entitled to replacement of the goods or a refund.

THE MISREPRESENTATION ACT 1967

This Act was intended to prevent retailers from making false statements about merchandise prior to its sale. Anyone who is misled can apply under the Act for compensation equal to the value of the loss incurred by relying on false information.

Misrepresentation may occur 'innocently' or 'fraudulently'. The former involves the making of statements that are genuinely believed to be true. Fraudulent misrepresentation, conversely, is false statements that are 'recklessly' or 'knowingly' made. Note, however, that false statements about merchandise, even if made unknowingly, may be considered by a court as fraudulent misrepresentation as the person selling the goods is assumed to possess expert knowledge about their quality and features.

OTHER CONSUMER PROTECTION LEGISLATION

The Unfair Contract Terms Act 1977 deals with the use of disclaimers and exemption clauses, restricting their use to certain specified circumstances. Thus, it is not permissible for a firm to make a general statement like 'anyone who enters these premises does so at their own risk' because this statement seeks to avoid responsibility for death or injury to employees or members of the public that might occur as a result of the firm's negligence, failure to implement statutory conditions or other fault.

Nevertheless, some exemption clauses are lawful, provided they are fair and reasonable. In assessing whether or not such a clause is 'reasonable', a court will consider:

- the bargaining positions of the parties;
- whether or not inducements (such as price reductions) were offered to the customer to accept the term;
- whether or not the goods were specially made for the customer;
- trade customs and whether or not the consumer should reasonably have known of the general existence of exemption clauses in a particular trade.

Coexisting with the 1977 Act are the Unfair Terms in Consumer Contracts Regulations 1994. These Regulations require that:

a contractual term which has not been individually negotiated shall be regarded as unfair and not binding on the consumer if, contrary to the requirement of good faith, it causes significant imbalance in the parties' contractual rights and obligations, to the detriment of the consumer.

This imposes a broader obligation than the 1977 Act as it is not restricted to exemption clauses. However, the Regulations only apply to 'consumers' and not to business-to-business deals or to 'individually negotiated' contracts.

■ Service contracts

The Supply of Goods and Services Act 1982 lays down consumers' rights in contracts that involve not only the supply of goods but also their installation and/or servicing.

As a result of the Act, the services (such as installation) supplied with physical goods must be carried out with reasonable skill and care to ensure that the goods supplied fulfil the purpose for which they were intended, and the services must be completed within a reasonable time. What constitutes 'a reasonable time' depends on the circumstances of the situation.

■ Weights and measures

Under the Weights and Measures Act 1985, it is a criminal offence for suppliers not to specify the quantities of most prepacked goods on their packets, tins or bottles.

The 1985 legislation is but one of a series of Weights and Measures Acts passed over the years. These have determined that:

- it is a criminal offence to give short weight or measure when supplying goods;
- responsibility for short-weight packages falls on the manufacturer or packager of goods rather than on the retailer;
- it is not necessary for each packet to be exactly the prescribed weight so long as the average weight of a batch of packets achieves the prescribed level.

■ Unsolicited goods

The Unsolicited Goods and Services Act 1971 states that where goods are delivered to someone who has not ordered them, then the customer is entitled to keep the goods after six months, provided that:

- the sender has not exercised their right to reclaim them within this period;
- the recipient has not undertaken to return the goods.

CONSUMER CREDIT

Credit arrangements in Britain are regulated by the Consumer Credit Act 1974, under which retail businesses that formally 'lend' (normally at interest) to their customers – by means of 'budget accounts', via a finance company, credit card charge accounts, personal loan accounts, payment by instalment agreements and so on – are subject to the Consumer Credit Act 1974 and thus require a licence (from the Office of Fair Trading) to grant credit.

Licences are only given to 'fit people', and trading without a licence is a criminal offence. However, the licencing provisions of the Act only apply to credit agreements between £50 and £15,000 in value. The Act forbids the charging of 'extortionate' interest and lays down many rules about how credit may be advertised. Note that normal trade credit that is expected to have been settled within three months is not affected by the Act.

Customers are entitled to the following information at the time of the transaction:

- the cash price of the goods, the amount of the deposit required and details of any security demanded;
- the value of the credit extended and its total cost, including the true annual percentage rate of interest;
- the timing and amount of repayments.

The customer must receive a copy of the credit agreement they have signed within seven days. If the customer entered a contract anywhere other than the firm's premises, they must receive two copies – one on signature and one by post within a further seven days, and the customer may then withdraw from the agreement without penalty within five days of receiving the second copy. Both copies must state the customer's right to cancel the agreement.

Any deposit must then be repaid and the goods collected by the supplying firm within three weeks These provisions do not apply if the agreement was signed on the premises of the supplying firm.

HIRE PURCHASE

Under the Act, a hirer has the right to terminate a hire purchase agreement at any time once installation charges plus half the total purchase price has been paid. If less than half the price has been paid, the hirer can be required to make up the balance to 50 per cent before cancelling the agreement or face a penalty. Hirers who settle early are entitled to a rebate on credit charges accrued under the deal.

Once a third of the purchase price has been remitted, the owner cannot repossess the goods without a court order. Note that these rules apply only to hire purchase and not to credit sales.

■ Exemptions

The Consumer Credit Act does not cover:

- borrowing by limited companies;
- mortgages;
- accounts that must be totally cleared each month (such as debts accrued on an American Express Card);
- loan arrangements involving fewer than five repayments.

The Act draws a crucial distinction between, on the one hand, 'debt or creditor–supplier' agreements – that is, where a finance company makes a loan for a specified purpose, such as buying a television set or motor vehicle, and, on the other, 'debtor–creditor' agreements, under which money is lent but for no specific purpose.

Under the former arrangements (sometimes called a 'purchaser agreement'), the company lending the money can be held equally liable with the supplier of the goods for any defects in them. This is why credit card companies such as Access or Barclaycard may be liable for the quality of the goods purchased using a credit card facility, whereas they are not liable for goods bought with cash drawn on a credit card. Hire purchase is a further example of a debtor–creditor–supplier deal. Bank overdrafts and personal loans are examples of the debtor–creditor relationship.

■ Licences

It is a criminal offence for unlicenced creditors to make loans, and only licenced sales people can make unsolicited calls on potential customers and offer credit terms. It is illegal to induce anyone under the age of 18 to enter a credit agreement.

Licences cost up to a couple of hundred pounds, depending on the size of the firm. All debt-collecting businesses, credit reference agencies, debt counsellors, plant hire enterprises and credit brokers (firms that introduce customers to hire purchase or leasing companies) require licences.

■ Extortionate agreements

If a court decides that a credit bargain is 'extortionate' (as sometimes happens in transactions with loan sharks, see Chapter 11), it may reschedule the repayments, alter the terms of the agreement or even set aside all or part of the debtor's obligations. In determining whether or not an agreement is extortionate, a court will examine:

- the 'principles of fair dealing';
- prevailing interest rates;
- whether or not the borrower was under pressure when the loan was agreed;
- the debtor's age, business experience, capacity and health;
- the degree of risk assumed and the lender's relationship with the borrower.

Debtors are entitled to repay any loan covered by the Act at any time and may be able to claim a rebate of interest (though this is not necessarily the case).

Creditors cannot take action against a borrower who fails to repay on time unless a 'notice of default' has been served on the debtor, giving seven days in which to pay up and outlining the consequences of not clearing the debt. Only if the debtor fails to respond to the notice of default may the lender then ask a court for an enforcement order (see Chapter 5) against the debt, and, even then, the court might give the debtor additional time to repay the loan.

■ Credit references

The Act stipulates that if you receive a written request from a customer to disclose the name and address of any credit reference agency you consulted for information about that customer's credit standing, then you must reveal this within seven working days whether or not a credit agreement resulted! However, the customer's request must be made within 28 days of the discussions (called 'antecedent negotiations') preceding the intended credit deal. If you receive a bad report on the customer from the credit reference agency, you are not obliged to disclose this; merely to provide the customer with the agency's name and address.

Having been given the details of the agency used, the customer is then entitled to demand from the agency full particulars of the records the agency holds on them (see below).

THE DATA PROTECTION ACT 1984

This Act requires computer users who store 'personal' data to register with the Data Protection Registrar. A small fee is payable; registration forms and further information are available from The Post Office.

When you register, you must declare what information you hold on people, its sources, uses and purpose and to whom you provide information taken from your system. Data subjects (the individuals about whom data is held) are legally entitled, on payment of a small fee, to demand a copy of any data held on them and this must be provided within 40 days of a written request. However, you can refuse to disclose information if:

- the request fee has not been paid;
- the data subject has not provided sufficient details for you to trace their records;
- requests are made too frequently by the same individual (bearing in mind the nature of the data) or if the requests are frivolous or vexatious in nature;
- you cannot relay the information without disclosing further infor-

mation that relates to another person who has not given their permission for its disclosure.

If your computer records contain information that can be linked to a specific living individual, then you must register your use of that data. Thus, file copies of word processed letters containing the addressee's name and address or a list of customers with the products they have purchased in the past or personnel records on staff must be declared.

There are certain exclusions in the Act. Computers that are used only for personal, family or household affairs are exempt, as are:

- mailing lists of names and addresses, provided no supplementary information is included (past customer purchases for example);
- company payrolls, as long as there is no intention to make the information available to other people and provided the only information listed is the name, address, date and amount of payment in respect of each employee;
- information on employee pensions;
- data held for national security purposes.

Only data held on 'automatically' processed systems is covered by the Act, so that manually operated systems (card indexes, for example) are not affected. 'Personal' information is defined as data relating to living people who 'can be identified from the information'. A sole trader is classified as a living 'person', but a limited company is not.

Failure to register leaves you open to prosecution. Registration itself is not automatic – it can be refused if the authorities consider that your reasons for wanting to hold the data are improper. Moreover, you are expected to observe eight internationally agreed principles on data protection, namely that the data be:

- obtained lawfully;
- used only for the purpose for which it is registered;
- disclosed only as specified at the time of registration;
- relevant to the purpose for which it is intended;
- accurate and up to date;
- available to data subjects on request;

- removed from files when it has served its purpose;
- adequately protected against loss or disclosure.

Note that if you pass computerised records to other organisations you are not obliged to inform the individuals detailed in the data transferred. Subjects can demand erasure or correction of information they know to be wrong, and are entitled to compensation if they suffer damage from inaccurate or inadequately protected data.

> *Suppliers are generally liable for defects in their products. You must be extremely vigilant where product liability is concerned, in respect both of your own products and those supplied to you by other firms.*

A data subject who feels unfairly treated may complain to the Data Protection Registrar who, following investigation, can issue to a data user an 'enforcement notice' demanding compliance with the provisions of the Act, or a 'deregistration notice' preventing the user from continuing to process personal data using an automatic system.

SUMMARY

Suppliers are generally liable for defects in their products. You must be extremely vigilant where product liability is concerned, in respect both of your own products and those supplied to you by other firms.

> *Not only must you not supply unsafe products, but you must not even possess them.*

A 'producer' can be a manufacturer, an importer, a distributor, extractor of raw materials, a firm that hires or lends the product to users or, indeed, any supplier of the item. Merely putting your business name or logo on a product might itself cause your firm to become liable if the goods turn out to be defective. Not only must you not supply unsafe products, but you must not even possess them. It is generally illegal to mislead consumers with respect to product price.

As the owner of a small business or SME, you need to be aware of the major provisions of the Sale and Supply of Goods Act and the Misrepresentation Act, which seeks to prevent businesses making false statements about their goods.

Consumer credit is regulated by the Consumer Credit Act. According to this, most businesses offering credit terms to their customers need to be licenced. There are also specific restrictions on how firms may offer credit to customers who are asked to sign credit contracts anywhere other than on the premises of the supplying firm.

✓ Checklist

☐ Have you checked to ensure that your product liability insurance is adequate, considering the implications of the Consumer Protection Act 1987?

☐ Do you ask major suppliers whether or not they are properly insured in respect of liability for defective products?

☐ Do you realise that you could be held liable for a defect in a product you sell even if you did not manufacture the item? If not, then reread this chapter.

☐ Have you examined your catalogues, price lists and other price indicators to establish that none of the prices you quote could be regarded as 'misleading'?

☐ Does your storeroom hold any unsafe products?

☐ If you are a retailer, what have you done to find out whether or not any of the goods you sell are unsafe?

☐ Is the way you describe your products in advertisements and other promotional materials accurate and not intended to misrepresent them to customers?

☐ If you sell on credit and do not have a licence, are you quite sure you do not require one?

☐ Have you registered under the Data Protection Act? If not, are you absolutely sure you don't need to register?

Restructuring for survival

1
2
3
4
5
6
7
8
9
10
11
12

INTRODUCTION

You have seen how you can cut costs and generally improve the efficiency of the operational aspects of the business. You should also by now have adopted a fresh and better attitude towards marketing, distribution, operations and promotional activities.

The next thing you must do is apply this new-found spirit of adventure to the overall composition of the firm. Thus, you need to ask some pointed questions about the adequacy of your existing legal structure and consider the alternatives that exist.

LEGAL STRUCTURES

So far, you will have traded as a single-person business, as a partnership or as a limited liability company. This chapter asks you to re-examine the suitability of the existing 'legal structure' (form of ownership) of the business and, perhaps, change to an alternative, more cost-effective and protective arrangement.

Some small businesses naively believe that becoming a private limited company is the be-all and end-all of legal structure. However, this is certainly not the case; limited liability is not necessarily the best way to conduct trade. On the other hand, the owner of a single-person business operating without limited liability (the technical term for such a firm is 'sole trader') stands to lose

Some small businesses naively believe that becoming a private limited company is the be-all and end-all of legal structure. However, this is certainly not the case.

their personal assets if the business fails. Choosing an appropriate legal structure is not always as straightforward as it first seems. Essentially, the choice depends on the:

- state of your cash flow;
- extent of your outstanding liabilities;
- costs and inconveniences of incorporation – that is, the process of becoming a limited company – in relation to the protection limited liability offers.

To understand these issues, we need to consider the advantages and disadvantages of your existing structural form.

THE SINGLE-PERSON BUSINESS TRADING WITHOUT
LIMITED LIABILITY

If you are a sole trader, you will not have had to bother with the legal formalities of forming a company, and your business affairs are entirely private except for your tax return. Moreover, you are free to diversify as and when you wish without being bound by company memoranda or articles of association (see below), so you can instantly exploit any business opportunities that emerge. Unfortunately, however, your liability for the business' debts is unlimited, which means that if you go bust, you must settle all these debts from your personal estate (house, car, furniture, money in your personal bank account and so on). Some of these difficulties can be overcome by altering your business' legal form, especially by forming a limited company and/or bringing in other people as stakeholders in the firm (creating a partnership, for instance), but there are many problems here of which you need to be aware.

PARTNERSHIP

Bringing in a partner can save an ailing business as a partner(s) might contribute skills or capital you do not possess. There are, however, several potential pitfalls, and entering into a partnership is not something to do without careful thought. The intended partner should be a person you get along with easily at work, though not necessarily someone you know well socially as a good social relationship does not always automatically translate into good working relations. Also, you really must have a

> *Bringing in a partner can save an ailing business as a partner(s) might contribute skills or capital you do not possess. There are, however, several potential pitfalls, and entering into a partnership is not something to do without careful thought.*

formal written partnership agreement that clearly establishes the precise obligations and rewards of each partner. Usually, partners will not want to invest in your business unless they have a say in how it is run, but this is not necessarily the case (see Note 1 at the end of the chapter). Sometimes people with money are prepared to invest in businesses without becoming involved in their management.

You can advertise for partners in the trade press, local newspapers, enterprise agencies, Chambers of Commerce or simply make discrete enquiries with existing business contacts.

■ Responsibility for debts

Partners in a business are jointly responsible (to the extent of their personal assets) for its debts. Moreover, a contract entered into by any one partner on behalf of the firm will bind the rest. If your partners have no assets when the business goes bust, the firm's creditors can come after you for the full amount they are owed.

■ Sleeping partners

There is an exception here. A partner who takes no part in management and does not enter contracts or sign cheques on behalf of the firm can obtain limited liability by registering the business as a 'limited partnership' with the registrar of companies at Companies House. Such a partner loses only the money they have invested in the partnership if the business fails. Remaining debts are the responsibility of other partners – at least one of which must, by law, have unlimited liability.

■ The Partnership Act 1890

Disputes within a partnership can arise over such things as:

- who is responsible for which activities;
- how much work each partner is to undertake;
- policy matters;
- the returns on money invested by partners in the business;
- distribution of profits;

and many other things.

A written agreement clarifying such issues is, therefore, essential, although many partnerships do not actually bother with this. In the absence of a written document, then – like it or not – the Partnership Act 1890 will apply to the firm. The major provisions of this Act are as follows:

- all partners shall share equally in the profits and losses of the business, and take equal shares of the partnership's capital assets upon its dissolution;
- partners are equally liable for the business' debts;
- contributions of capital over and above those the partners initially agreed to pay should attract interest at the rate of 5 per cent;
- partners shall share equally in management, and be rewarded via shares in the profit of the enterprise (no salaries are paid);
- new partners may not be admitted unless all the existing partners give their consent;
- disputes must be settled by majority vote, unless a change in the nature of the partnership's business is envisaged, in which case a unanimous decision is required.

Note, importantly, that as a partnership is a relationship between people, it automatically ceases on the death of any one partner. If the business is to continue following a partner's death, an entirely new partnership must be formed.

Be sure you understand the legal implications of partnership before you take a partner. That person becomes an agent of the firm and can bind it contractually without your knowledge or prior consent, and you are personally liable for debts thus incurred. Your partner can buy goods for the business, sell its assets and borrow money on its behalf. If you leave the partnership or retire, you are still responsible for the debts accumulated while you were a member of the firm.

Sometimes, sole traders take as partners existing employees whose past contributions to the firm have been particularly valuable. Note, however, that the kinds of personal qualities that are excellent for being a good employee – working under someone else's direction – are not necessarily identical to those found in successful entrepreneurs. Perhaps, therefore, an ex-employee should begin as a 'junior' partner, with restricted powers and responsibilities, prior to their promotion to a 'senior partner' role.

You can have up to 20 partners for a non-banking business, 10 if banking is involved and any number if the partnership is 'professional' in nature – solicitors, for example. The extent of your partners' powers should be embodied in a written 'partnership deed' specifying:

- the precise duties of each partner, whether or not they can sign cheques and, if so, up to what amount;
- the basis on which partners shall contribute capital and their returns on such investments;
- rules for admission of new partners and the age at which partners shall retire;
- how profits shall be divided.

The deed can be tailor-made to side-step some of the inconveniences of partnership (that partnerships automatically end on the death, resignation or retirement of any one partner, for instance). Moreover, a retiring partner need not be liable for previously accumulated partnership debts provided a special 'contract of novation' exists between themselves, existing partners, creditors and a new partner entering the firm. Novation means the substitution of a new legal obligation for an old one with the consent of all parties. Here, the new entrant contracts to 'take the place' of the retiring partner as far as existing debts are concerned.

A problem confronting retiring or resigning partners is that, in certain circumstances, they can be deemed liable for debts incurred after they leave the firm. This is because a creditor who continuously does business with a partnership is entitled to assume that all its 'apparent' members are still there until formally notified of the change. Thus, it is essential that if you leave a partnership, you notify all existing customers and suppliers at once. Also, you can advertise your resignation in the *London Gazette*, which officially gives notice of your withdrawal to anyone who has not previously dealt with the firm.

Ultimately, a partnership will succeed or fail depending on the energy, skills, mutual trust, competence, commitment and cooperation of the partners. A good partner is an invaluable asset. They can be a source of emotional support as well as financial assistance. Bad partners, however, can ruin the firm, so be careful.

LIMITED LIABILITY

The overwhelming disability attached to trading in ordinary partnership or alone is that, so far as your creditors are concerned, you cannot separate your firm's assets – the premises, equipment, stock, cash in hand, vehicles and so on of the business – from your own private property, which you must use to meet the firm's debts if the business fails.

Normally, a solvent small business or SME with a high cash flow or that enters the occasional *ad hoc* high-value transaction should seek limited liability. Suppose, for example, that your monthly income is £70,000, with outgoings of £65,000 per month, giving you £5,000 per month profit – £60,000 per year. Obviously, you have a profitable business. However, suppose something happens to prevent you realising, albeit temporarily, your sales (such as a strike among input suppliers, liquidation of a major distributor, an exceptionally severe seasonal decline). You have already entered contracts for the supply of inputs – such as labour, raw materials, rent on the premises and so on – and are legally committed to settling these debts, yet your income has ceased!

After 4 weeks, you owe £65,000, after 8 weeks, £130,000, and nearly £200,000 after 3 months! By now, your creditors are issuing writs and the business is collapsing – leaving you saddled with a vast amount of debt that you are personally obliged to clear up.

■ What limited liability is

To avoid this possibility, you could form a limited company. This enables you to restrict your personal liability for the business' debts to the amount you have invested in the company (usually a nominal £100), provided the company was formed before the debts were incurred.

Effectively, you become a shareholder in your own firm, and are liable for its debts only to the value of your shares. Creditors can claim from the firm's assets (of which your £100 share capital is a part), but they cannot take any of your personal goods because, in law, the business is an entirely different person to yourself – you happened to invest in it, you were its employee, but, apart from your shareholding, you are not responsible for its debts!

■ Debts previously incurred

Do not imagine you can avoid liability for debts already run up while you were a sole trader or in partnership simply by forming a company. Debts assumed in your own name (or business name) remain in your own name and are not taken over by the company, which, in law, is a completely different and independent business to the one that existed before. Only debts invoiced to the company after its formation are covered by the principle of limited liability.

■ Personal guarantees

Note that banks (and sometimes even trade creditors) ask directors of limited companies to give personal financial guarantees for loans or major credit contracts. If you have signed such guarantees and if the bank or one or two large creditors constitutes the great bulk of your outstanding debt, then there is very little point in forming a limited company in the first place. Indeed, you could actually be worse off under such an arrangement because the guarantee could involve a particular personal asset (your house, for instance) that, if seized, could cause your family great emotional as well as financial distress. Nor will your death cancel the guarantee as the asset must still be surrendered, even if its loss results in your surviving relatives becoming destitute (typically your spouse has to sign the guarantee as well if there is any question of joint or family ownership).

Another common misconception about limited companies is the idea that their directors are not personally liable for damage caused by allowing trading to continue despite knowing the company is already, or about to become, insolvent. The 1986 Insolvency Act has considerably strengthened creditors' ability to claim from company shareholders' personal estates.

■ Fraudulent and wrongful trading

Personal liability arises in either of the following two circumstances.

Wrongful trading

A shareholder who helps manage a company is liable for its debts if the company continues to trade prior to liquidation while they knew, or ought to have known, there was no reasonable prospect of avoiding insolvency. Wrongful trading is not fraud (that is, deliberately trading in order to obtain benefit, despite knowing the business is about to fail). Rather, it is the consequence of 'poor judgement'.

Courts will ask, 'What should a prudent, knowledgeable person have done in the circumstances?' If a court considers that continuation of the business for a few extra weeks or months might have enabled settlement of a few more debts, no personal liability arises.

Fraudulent trading

This means deliberate bad judgement (that is, carrying on the business intending to put its creditors in a worse position).

A court might then seek to identify the individuals responsible for the company's fraudulent trading.

Personal liability can be avoided in such circumstances if you can prove you took 'all reasonable precautions' to avoid potential problems. In practice, this might require your demonstrating that you:

- regularly checked the financial state of the business;
- checked the accuracy of management control information, including accounting data;
- planned future activities;
- did not give preferential treatment to any one creditor (who might be connected to the director in question) at the expense of others;
- took proper professional advice – for example, from a qualified accountant.

Objects of the company

You have to ensure, moreover, that all your business transactions are covered by the memorandum of association (see below) of the company you form. If you buy a company 'off the peg' (usually costing about £100), check the 'objects' clause in the memorandum. This states the purpose of the business and the activities it exists to undertake. A garage business, for instance, needs an objects clause specifying activities such as the purchase and sale of vehicles, petrol, motor accessories, servicing of vehicles and so on.

If your off-the-peg company (acquired perhaps via mail order advertised in the trade press) has an objects clause designed for a business selling fish and chips, then you might not be able to enforce contracts that relate to the garage! Such contracts are called *ultra vires* contracts, meaning that a fish and chip shop (the legal personality and purpose of which is established in the objects clause) has no contractual powers to be dealing in anything other than fish and chips (unless the company's objects have been drafted in such general terms that virtually any trading activity is covered – if you have a company, check whether this is so in your own case).

■ Other problems with companies

Two further problems exist.

- You must prepare annually a profit and loss account and balance sheet audited by a qualified accountant (to whom you will have to pay a fee) and deposit these with the Registrar of Companies.
- When the business becomes a limited company, you become an employee of the company (which has its own separate legal identity) and, thus, liable to PAYE and Class 1 National Insurance contributions. Additionally, the company must also pay employers' NI contributions as an employer in its own right! Note, however, that you become entitled to unemployment benefit if the company fails.

A payment by the company to you as a director is a tax-deductible business expense as far as the company is concerned, but counts as taxable income for you personally. Profits earned by the company attract corporation tax, the rate of which varies from time to time.

There are no restrictions as to how much a sole trader may withdraw from their business. Limited companies may pay salaries to directors, but company law generally prohibits directors receiving company loans. Note that, importantly, companies are allowed to sell and buy back their own shares in certain circumstances, thus enabling venture capital financing (see Note 1) to occur (though the company's articles of association must clearly state that this may take place)

Companies with five or fewer shareholders (or which are controlled by any number of directors who are also shareholders) are called 'close companies'. The tax authorities might attribute the investment income of a close company to shareholders – that is, tax officers will assume that investment income is the result of shareholders using the company as a 'money box' for the purpose of only paying corporation tax, (whereas if they invested similar amounts as individuals they might be liable for much higher personal rates of tax).

COMPANY FORMATION

Many sole traders are put off the idea of forming a company by the legal jargon involved. Do not be afraid of legal terms – it is the costs and benefits regarding risk, tax, National Insurance contributions and cash flow considerations that should determine your choice of legal structure, not the fear of legalistic terminology.

Having read the above, you should understand the fundamental issues involved and feel reasonably confident about buying a company off the peg. Such companies are usually satisfactory, provided your business does not undertake unusual or highly specialist activities and you check to ensure that the objects clause of a company purchased in this way actually meets your trading needs. A ready-made company is instantly available and cheap, and even if the name of the company is not exactly to your liking it can be changed on payment of a small fee (provided the name chosen is not obscene, offensive or illegal, and provided no other company with that name has already been registered).

Otherwise, the details of company formation need not be your concern as the registration agent will do most of the work. I assume that as a small business you would not want to consider becoming a public company, which needs £50,000 of share capital at least, and that you wish to maintain your personal and direct control of the firm. Thus, a 'private' company is probably appropriate for your needs. These require just one or more shareholders, one director (normally yourself) and a company secretary who might perhaps be another shareholder or your accountant. A company secretary is an important officer of the company – responsible for transmitting various documents to the Registrar of Companies, communicating formally with shareholders on the company's behalf and enabling the company to operate in accordance with the law - and not a shorthand typist as the name might suggest.

Briefly, companies are formed by depositing certain documents with the Registrar of Companies and paying a registration fee (currently £50).

COMPANY DOCUMENTS

These documents are:

- the memorandum of association;
- articles of association – that is, the internal 'rules' of the company regarding shareholders' voting rights and so on;
- a statement of how many shares the company can issue (usually £100) plus details of the company's name, address, shareholders, directors, etc.

The former can be obtained through the post from a registration agent who will already possess hundreds of ready-formed companies on file. The agent finds a company suitable for your business and sells the package of its documents to you for, currently, £100 to £200. Articles of association are not normally included in the package because there is no legal requirement that they be deposited. If they are not, courts simply assume that the specimen articles contained in the Companies (Tables A to F) Regulations 1985 (issued under the Companies Act 1985) apply to the company. All you have to do is complete – together with one other person – two forms in order to change the director and secretary of the company and the company's registered address from those already on file.

Buying a company 'off the peg' is a suitable option for new businesses or where the firm being converted into a company owns very little property. If, however, the business already possesses land or other substantial assets that are to be passed on to the new company or if complicated leases on premises are involved, then expert advice from a lawyer or chartered accountant is usually required.

RUNNING A COMPANY

On its formation, you receive from the registration agent (or your accountant or solicitor) the following items, in addition to the company's memorandum of association, a Certificate of Incorporation (a sort of 'birth certificate' for the company), plus some share certificates that can be used to issue or transfer company shares. If the company is purchased off the peg, you also receive the letters of resignation of the first director and secretary (that is, the agents who set the company up).

To run the company, you (or the company secretary) must record changes in directors, share transfers, debenture issues, mortgages and charges, and transmit this information to the Registrar at Companies House. At the end of each financial year, the company must submit its final accounts (approved by the company's directors and externally audited) to the Registrar. These accounts must be accompanied by a directors' report outlining:

- any major events occurring during the previous 12 months;
- lists of directors' names, addresses and financial interests in the company;
- any political or charitable donations made by the company in excess of £200.

The report must be circulated to all shareholders prior to the company's annual general meeting.

■ Exemptions

'Small' companies with annual turnovers and asset values not exceeding certain thresholds and fewer than 50 employees need not file directors' reports, but must still produce them and send copies to shareholders, and the reports must inform shareholders that the company has utilised the exemption. A business satisfying the 'small company' criteria is also exempt from filing its profit and loss account with the Registrar (although a balance sheet must still be deposited).

■ Being a director

As a director of a limited company you incur certain legal obligations. Also, restrictions exist on who may become directors in the first place, in particular:

- a person cannot be a company's sole director and its secretary;
- undischarged bankrupts may not become company directors;
- directors' spouses and children must declare their holdings of the company's shares and/or debentures;
- directors must declare any directorships of other UK companies;
- if a director has an external business interest in a contract that the company is considering entering into, then they must declare this to the Board meeting at which the contract is discussed;
- directors' contracts of employment (including details of remuneration) must be available for inspection by shareholders;
- on a director's resignation, any compensation paid to that person for loss of of fice must be approved by shareholders.

ACQUIRING OTHER FIRMS

Many factors may cause you to want another firm – control over supplies, integration of processes, acquisition of extra plant and equipment, access to distribution channels, building up of transport facilities and so on. If a competitor is the major source of yor difficulties, you may want to consider submitting an offer for taking over that business (the deal being financed by a loan secured against the assets of the acquired firm). A common stimulus to expansion by takeover is the need to diversify into new products and market segments. The business you acquire may possess the equipment necessary for producing new (as far as you are concerned) products and already employ staff with the relevant skills. It might also own brand names, logos and so on already familiar in the markets you intend to enter.

■ Problems with acquisitions

There are, of course, many potential pitfalls attached to acquisitions, so you must analyse the products, markets and competitors of the firm you have in mind carefully. Common difficulties include the following.

- Lack of experience and technical knowledge of the line or business of the firm you intend acquiring. Possibly you can take over existing employees when you buy the firm, but they might soon leave, or your working methods and approaches to problems might differ, causing difficulties on both sides.
- Sudden changes in market conditions or the emergence of new competitors following the acquisition.
- Inability to coordinate the work of two businesses at the same time. Running two, or more, firms simultaneously requires considerable managerial expertise and attention to the detail of a wide range of issues. Techniques applicable to one of your businesses might not be relevant to the other. At worst, all the problems you have experienced in your first business will be repeated in the second.
- The need to gather management control information (for example, rates of return, operating data, information on environmental conditions) for two businesses instead of one.

Specialist advice may be needed on particular issues, especially if anyone is to be made redundant at the time of the takeover (normally the vendor is responsible for making redundancy payments, although you need a written indemnity from the vendor confirming their liability in this respect) or if patents, registered trademarks, service contracts or licences have to be transferred. The dismissal of employees is automatically unfair (see Chapter 6) if the transfer of ownership of a business is the sole or main reason for the sacking.

■ Need for caution

Whatever you do, never sign an undertaking that you will honour the acquired business' previously accumulated debts – these are entirely the responsibility of the owner(s) of the old firm. In purchasing the business, you have effectively created a completely new firm as far as creditors are concerned, so make clear the change of ownership to suppliers as you receive invoices. All existing liabilities should, of course, be settled at the time ownership is transferred.

Remember, too, that if you choose not to conduct the acquired business under your own name (say, by continuing to trade under the business' previous title), you are legally obliged to state your name clearly on all business documents and correspondence.

■ The danger of new competition

Note that the person who sold you the new business is normally quite free to set up in competition against you. This possibility might perhaps be pre-empted by insisting that the vendor sign an agreement not to compete with you within a certain area for so many years, but such contracts are complicated in their interpretation and could be challenged in court. Generally, courts dislike such agreements (although they are not illegal) on the grounds that they are 'contrary to the public interest' and liable, therefore, to be declared void if one of the parties so desires.

■ The need for indemnity

If the business you acquire is already a limited company, then, because a company is a legal 'person' in its own right, its liability for debts, faults in past output, pension schemes for employees and so on continue regardless of who is the majority shareholder. In this case, however, you are protected by the doctrine of limited liability and so are not personally responsible for the company's debts beyond the value of your shareholding. Ensure, nevertheless, that all liabilities have been settled before taking a majority of shares. It might also be wise to have a solicitor obtain a personal indemnity against previously accumulated company debts from the last majority shareholder.

Otherwise, you might discover, to your horror, that the previous owner had run up large debts in the company's name immediately before the share transfer, resulting, perhaps, in creditors forcing liquidation of the company just after you take possession.

A REVIVAL PLAN

Detail your intentions for revitalising the business in a written plan. This will be useful for negotiating with bank managers, creditors, landlords, local authority business development officers and others, and the discipline of writing it forces you to clarify your thoughts and investigate key issues properly. Banks, in particular, will want to see objective, written analyses and plans for action before lending you money. Written plans also make it easier for outsiders to understand and evaluate your proposals, and they provide a basis for further discussions. You can also use the plan to monitor your progress as you develop the business in its new form.

> *Detail your intentions for revitalising the business in a written plan. This will be useful for negotiating with bank managers, creditors, landlords, local authority business development officers and others, and the discipline of writing it forces you to clarify your thoughts and investigate key issues properly.*

■ Layout

The plan should have:

- a beginning – stating why you are initiating change;
- a middle – outlining how you intend improving the business;
- an end – specifying detailed objectives.

Start the plan with an introduction outlining the origin of the business, what impelled you initially to set it up, how it has developed and the barriers and problems that have temporarily (you hope) interrupted its successful expansion – for example, a technical change, emergence of a new competitor who has perhaps unfairly slashed prices, thus forcing you to look to other markets, labour shortages and so on.

■ The body of the plan

Then you need headed sections explaining the changes in production methods, supply arrangements, labour procurement, organisation structures and so on that you intend to implement, plus outlines of any major cost-cutting exercises already undertaken.

Follow this with some headed paragraphs on how you will market your new, altered, modified or existing products. List their selling points, who will buy them, where, and why. Describe the following:

- the present state of the competition;
- any market research undertaken – however basic;
- which market segments you intend to tackle;
- your pricing strategy, specifying discount structures and credit policies, with full justifications.

Emphasise the strengths of your plan rather than its weaknesses. However, recognise that if major shortcomings exist, outsiders will almost certainly spot them so you might as well point them out from the beginning, but then spell out how you intend to overcome the difficulties.

Now state your basic assumptions about the nature of future environments, including:

- tax regimes;
- consumer protection and other laws;
- production techniques;
- public tastes and fashions;
- how significant environmental change might affect the business.

Outline intended promotional programmes, mentioning the techniques (coupons, premium offers, competitions, for example) to be adopted.

The plan should detail your intentions for dealing with existing inadequacies in distribution channels (breakages, deterioration of goods, high packaging costs and so on) specifying the measures you mean to apply to improve the system – such as security systems to prevent pilfering, new warehousing arrangements, different outlets, introduction of a mail order service, purchase or sale of delivery vehicles.

Other important matters to be dealt with in the plan are:

- changes in key employees, and the qualifications, skills and experiences of new entrants;
- locations of competitors, and how many new competitors you expect in the future;
- a recent or proposed change in legal structure – for example, from a partnership to a limited company and the reasons for this;
- contingency plans stating alternative sources of supply (following a strike affecting a major supplier, for example), who will take control if you fall ill, how you will cope with bad weather and how you will handle other emergencies that might have a detrimental effect on your firm.

It is important that you have a contingency plan for dealing with serious equipment breakdowns. You might, for example, enter a mutual arrangement with another firm whereby you each agree to make your plant and machinery available to the other for night shift working for a limited period in the event of a dire emergency. (Your employees must, of course, be informed of and agree to such an arrangement.) Regularly check the current costs and availabilities of leased equipment that could be used in these circumstances. Also, keep an eye open for possibilities for short-term subcontracting.

Actual or proposed changes in premises require prominent attention being given to them in the main part of the document. Outline the predicted benefits of the alterations, the extra facilities available, lower costs and so on.

■ Financial matters

Outsiders are primarily interested in the financial worth of the business and its future trading prospects. List the firm's:

- assets and liabilities;
- key financial ratios;
- breakeven points for various output prices.

Mention major contracts presently being undertaken, the current state of trade and where your custom is mainly located. Append to the plan a comprehensive 12-month cash flow forecast and an estimated end of year profit and loss account. Then, specify the additional resources (machines and equipment, new premises, extra working capital and so on) necessary for successful operations and where you want the money to come from.

Whenever possible, support your objectives with evidence of the likelihood of their success; appending documents, statistics, lists of potential buyers and other such relevant details. Say precisely how you expect targets to be attained, but express cautious realism when assessing the probability of their achievement.

If you are looking for a substantial bank loan, the bank will want to be sure that the revitalised business can generate sufficient revenues to repay loan capital and interest at appropriate intervals. The bank will also need to know the extent of your personal means and of your own investment in the business. Accordingly, a business revival plan that is to be used to raise finance for the company must contain a list of your personal assets – property, vehicles, house contents, stocks and shares, insurance policies and so on – that could act as security against a loan.

The section on objectives should state definite sales targets, cost-reduction programmes, gross and net margins, and target cash in flows. If you intend introducing new products, specify timetables for their launches. Whenever possible, support your objectives with evidence of the likelihood of their success; appending documents, statistics, lists of potential buyers and other such relevant details.

Say precisely how you expect targets to be attained, but express cautious realism when assessing the probability of their achievement. Quote figures for expected market share, turnover, profit contributions by market segment, product line, customer location and so on.

SUMMARY

Businesses cannot operate effectively in the longer term unless they stand on firm and appropriate organisational and legal foundations. If you are a sole trader, consider the feasibility of taking a partner. Seriously consider whether or not limited liability would

be appropriate for your firm. If you already trade as a limited company, yet still have to provide personal guarantees for all major loans and credit transactions, then ask yourself whether or not the costs and inconvenience of operating a limited company are really worth while.

Advantages and disadvantages are attached to each of the various forms of business ownership. Which to choose depends on the circumstances of the enterprise and how you want it to develop. Note, however, that it is not possible to avoid personal liability for a business' existing debts simply by converting the firm into a company halfway through its life as all debts incurred prior to the conversion remain with you.

Possibly, your business can be improved by acquiring another firm. This might enable you to integrate production processes, obtain much-needed plant and equipment, rationalise distribution channels, and so on. Yet, many difficulties are attached to mergers and acquisitions, so you must take great care not to bite off more than you can chew.

All your proposals for revitalising the business should be embodied in a written revival plan, with lots of headings and a comprehensive statement of the various aspects of your firm's present and likely future operations.

✓ Checklist

☐ How many people do you know who might be prepared to inject fresh capital into your firm?

☐ If you go bust tomorrow, how much will your business owe, and to what extent are these liabilities covered by the realisable assets of the firm?

☐ Do you understand the difference between wrongful trading and fraudulent trading?

☐ Can you list three benefits of your acquiring another firm?

☐ Do you feel you have the experience, technical knowledge and energy to run two businesses at the same time?

☐ Have you prepared a formal plan for reviving your business?

☐ What are the three major business objectives you wish to achieve within the next three years?

☐ What are the major barriers that might prevent you achieving these objectives?

☐ List two significant technological developments that may occur in your industry over the next five years and state how they will affect your firm.

☐ What would happen to your business if its senior employee were to quit next week?

Note

1. Venture financing means that an outside body (such as a merchant bank) buys shares in your business in order to inject capital, takes a big share of the profits in return, then sells the shares back to the company for an agreed price at a predetermined future date.

The wolf is at the door

1
2
3
4
5
6
7
8
9
10
11
12

INTRODUCTION

So far, I have concentrated on practical measures for turning around businesses which, although they have experienced problems and thus achieved only modest rates of return, are nevertheless fully solvent in the medium, if not the short, term. How, though, should you proceed when confronted with really serious financial difficulties, when you haven't any money at all and are being hounded by creditors?

This chapter is intended to help you cope with an immediate and desperate cash flow deficit. It outlines a plan of emergency action to use when you simply cannot honour your outstanding bills. Drastic measures are involved – typically requiring the surrender, at a loss, of capital assets. Yet, the forfeit of assets, in association with other crisis policies, may be the only way to save the firm – indeed, the only way you can avoid personal bankruptcy and the consequent seizure of your private estate.

TAKING STOCK

In this situation you should list all the amounts you owe in order – not of when they fall due, but, rather, in terms of the seriousness of the consequences of various creditors taking action to recover outstanding balances. For instance, the detrimental effects of a supplier putting you on to a 'cash with order' basis until you settle your credit account might not be as severe as, say, having your gas or electricity cut off during the winter. Conversely, you might be able to do

> *You should list all the amounts you owe in order – not of when they fall due, but, rather, in terms of the seriousness of the consequences of various creditors taking action to recover outstanding balances.*

without gas-fired central heating for a month or two in the summer, but it is unlikely (though not entirely impossible) that you could do without a telephone.

Ruthless realism is required. Impose a strict embargo on all capital expenditure and look for fast ways of raising cash. If you operate a very small, single-person business, you might be able to take a paid job for a few weeks and run the business part-time. This is exhausting, but might just be feasible in the very short term, and at least it keeps your business alive.

Sell all your surplus assets (including unused stock) and, wherever possible, replace purchased capital assets (vehicles, equipment and so on) that you can liquidate for cash with leased items. Make sure you are fully informed of all revenue the moment it arrives, of needs for immediate expenditures (minimum gas or electricity payments needed to avoid being cut off, for example) and the expected dates of other necessary spending.

Specific policies are needed in each of the following areas.

PREMISES

While sale and leaseback (see Chapter 4) is obviously an appropriate medium-term capital-raising measure for businesses that own their premises, it takes time to organise and involves substantial expenditures (solicitors and valuation fees, for example). In buying your premises, you will almost certainly have financed the transaction by means of a mortgage, probably via a bank or building society. A bank will have lent to you – against the security of the business' premises and/or other assets – for anything up to 20 years. Building society loans are available for business premises and are similarly secured, but usually they are only available to people who have already paid off most of their private household mortgages.

■ Increasing an existing mortgage

If to date you have a good mortgage repayment record, the best solution may be to approach the mortgagor of the premises and request an increase in the size of the mortgage, and/or an extension in the period of the loan, with the bigger mortgage being secured against the building's higher current market worth. Such an injection of finance might even enable you to pay off all your outstanding business debts and totally reconstitute the firm. Thus, the need for alternative, more draconian, measures is overcome. Note, too, that if presently you run a large overdraft, then your borrowings are extremely expensive in view of the high interest rates on overdraft loans. It will pay you, therefore, to swap overdrafts (and any other high-cost short-term borrowing) for higher mortgage repayments, which have a significantly lower interest rate. Indeed, a substantial lengthening of the repayment period might stretch out the repayments on a higher mortgage to the extent that the monthly amount payable actually falls. Also,

> *If to date you have a good mortgage repayment record, the best solution may be to approach the mortgagor of the premises and request an increase in the size of the mortgage, and/or an extension in the period of the loan, with the bigger mortgage being secured against the building's higher current market worth.*

you will, of course, have realised a substantial capital sum.

Mortgagors will usually listen to small business and SME owners who wish to enter into this type of arrangement because most lenders realise that a freshly constituted firm is far better able to repay a mortgage (and is therefore a safer lending proposition) than a run-down business constantly struggling to cope with high-priced debts!

Banks and building societies can, and do, reclaim property in the last resort, but generally wish to avoid the legal and administrative costs, inconvenience and unpleasantness associated with this. Thus, they might respond sympathetically to a request for a higher mortgage that helps prevent such an eventuality. Remember, however, that you can do this only once. If you squander the benefits of a higher mortgage, you will not be given a second chance.

■ Mortgage arrears

A bank or building society may be prepared to suspend or reduce your capital and/or interest repayments temporarily. It is better to ask than simply await a summons to court in respect of a possession order. Do not think you are better off allowing 'nature to take its course' with a court order, because substantial legal, administrative and valuation costs will be involved in the sale of the property following its repossession. All these costs are deducted from the sale proceeds before the sum raised is applied to the outstanding balance. Also, the mortgagor will be seeking a quick sale and thus might sell to the first purchaser who comes along, even if only a low price is offered.

Remember always that banks and building societies want to avoid unpleasant and administratively troublesome repossession proceedings. Mortgagors invariably prefer to accommodate the unfortunate circumstances afflicting bona fide borrowers than to evict, even when legally entitled to do so, provided the mortgagee demonstrates a genuine willingness to repay the arrears. In assessing your commitment, the lender (a bank, say) will consider:

- how quickly you came to see them after getting into financial difficulties;
- whether or not the source of your cash flow problems lies in your own negligence or incompetence, or in external and, perhaps, unavoidable events;
- the extent and nature of the measures you have implemented to revitalise the business and the likelihood of their success;
- whether or not you ignored earlier warning letters – other than, perhaps, the first couple.

The longer you delay discussing your predicament with the lender the worse it is for you. Note, in particular, that the issue of a court order in relation to premises may lead to your name appearing on a list of general bad payers (many credit agencies collect information on people against whom such court orders have been issued), resulting possibly in your not being able to obtain business, or indeed personal, credit in the future.

■ Subletting

Subletting part of your premises provides a quick source of income, though certain costs and inconveniences are necessarily involved. For example, separate telephone lines must be installed, office partitions erected and there is the additional expense of advertising for tenants. Note that extra planning permission may be needed before conversion occurs.

▣ *Property conversion*

Significant economies of scale are available from property conversion. It might be only a little more expensive to subdivide an entire large building into small lettable units than it would be to undertake all the work necessary just to fit out your own firm. Also the rent from subletting the units you have created might pay not only for the conversion work itself but also for the essential maintenance and repairs that you would have had to undertake in any event.

Even if your premises are leased and the lease does not permit subletting, it may still be worth approaching the landlord to ask for special permission to convert the premises and sublet. After all, you are offering to undertake the conversion into smaller, possibly more marketable units at your own expense, and you would not be doing this if the demand for smaller units did not exist.

■ Make room to sublet

If you have recently expanded the business, you may feel that you cannot possibly make room to sublet. However, expansion does not inevitably lead to greater space utilisation. It may make sense to sublet, therefore, provided that:

- you have efficient systems for dealing with goods inward, stock control and finished goods awaiting dispatch – so that large areas are not tied up accommodating excessive amounts of idle stock;
- you take the trouble to reorganise, tidy up the existing premises and generally conserve the floor space needed for your own operations.

■ Check local rents

Of course, conversion and subletting should only be considered if local rent levels and user demand are sufficient to make the exercise financially worth while. Accordingly, you should regularly collect information from local estate agents and others on current rentals for nearby premises of varying quality and size.

RENT AND RATES

A business that rents its premises will have a lease or a licence (see Note 2) that determines the precise conditions of its tenancy. Most rented premises are let under a lease of between 3 and 20 years, although shorter-term agreements are possible, providing, perhaps, for as little as a week's notice to terminate the contract. However, these very short-term leases are not common because of their unpopularity with tenants, who dislike them on account of their inherent lack of tenant security.

Possibly the most tempting thing to do when you cannot pay all your outstanding bills is to miss paying this month's rent. Unfortunately, arrears can soon build up to the point where they become a major threat to the survival of the firm.

■ Rent arrears

Possibly the most tempting thing to do when you cannot pay all your outstanding bills is to miss paying this month's rent. Unfortunately, arrears can soon build up to the point where they become a major threat to the survival of the firm. Also, if you fall too far behind, the landlord will seek to repossess the premises.

■ Danger of eviction

Legally, it is much easier to evict someone from business premises than it is from a household. Indeed, if you are well behind with the rent on business premises, then a court has little option but to grant the landlord an eviction order, which, if it is not obeyed, will quickly be followed by forcible eviction by court officers.

This rapid eviction need not occur, however, if you are 'in dispute' with the landlord regarding a lease 'covenant'. Lease covenants involve matters such as:

- who is responsible for the maintenance and repair of the property – for instance, you might be justified in withholding rent if necessary repairs have not been undertaken by a landlord who is contractually liable for their execution;
- who is responsible for the payment of rates;
- the details of procedures for repossession.

■ The lease

Three aspects of a lease are especially important for a small business in financial difficulties:

- rent reviews;
- subletting clauses;
- surrender arrangements.

Most longer-term leases (in excess of two or three years, say) contain a rent review clause.

■ *Rent reviews*

The size of the rent increase associated with the clause is subject to negotiation, normally based on some published index of changes in property prices or a general measure of inflation. A rent review can come as a nasty shock to a recently established business that did not anticipate a big rent increase early in its occupation of a building. Look carefully at your lease to identify any such provision, and budget generously for possible rent increases.

■ *Subletting*

Look carefully through your lease for any clause that might prevent you subletting parts of the premises in times of crisis.

■ *Surrender arrangements*

The third potential source of difficulty – lease clauses that prevent you terminating the lease quickly or assigning it to another business without penalty – can be most distressing. Landlords normally insist that tenants see out their tenancies or pay full compensation for early surrender. Check your lease to ensure you fully understand its surrender provisions.

■ Avoiding eviction

If you are evicted for rent arrears, you will have difficulties in finding new premises because landlords (or estate agents acting on their behalf) usually want to know your previous location and why you left that building. The physical move attached to eviction may itself disrupt your existing business. Eviction, therefore, must always be avoided.

When you become a long way behind with the rent, explain to the landlord or managing agent the reasons for your not being able to meet your obligations, emphasising the positive measures you are taking to revitalise the business. Landlords are anxious not to incur the administrative and legal costs attached to eviction and the inevitable loss of the accumulated rent already owing. Hence, they might react more sympathetically to a reasonable proposal for slowly reducing the arrears than you might initially have expected.

Make an offer

The process of reporting your difficulties to the landlord may take quite a long time, thus giving the business a limited period in which to recover, especially if the landlord uses an agent to collect the rent. Offer to pay your arrears by increasing your monthly rent by a small amount, starting a couple of months from now. This presents the landlord with a tangible alternative to having to write off the debt as the arrears cease to accumulate and you demonstrate your good faith to the landlord.

If your premises are too big and the lease forbids you to sublet, point out to the landlord how the business may collapse, leaving the landlord with a large unsettled account if the lease is not altered. Perhaps you could sublet and pay the landlord a percentage of the incoming rent or simply redefine the boundaries of your tenancy (at a lower rent) thus allowing the landlord to let other parts of your existing premises.

The costs of eviction

Emphasise the costs to the landlord of not accommodating your needs. Tenants of local authority premises sometimes have an advantage here because local authorities are subject to democratic control and you can appeal directly to your local councillor if the authority threatens to evict. In fact, few councils will actually put a small business on to the streets (except as a very last resort), provided the firm demonstrates its determination to stop rent arrears from accumulating further. Indeed, a local council may even help you find cheaper alternative accommodation.

Private landlords will not normally allow large arrears to build up and will quickly seek an eviction order once they suspect that a tenant is insolvent. On receipt of a court summons, you must first decide whether or not to contest the action. Either you 'admit' the landlord's allegation of non-payment or you 'defend' your position. Grounds for defence include:

- disagreement over how much is owed;
- counterclaims for emergency repairs you needed to undertake at your own expense despite their being the landlord's responsibility;
- the landlord's failure to maintain the building properly.

Following the delivery of a contested summons, go to the landlord with another offer. State how much you can afford to pay each month and contrast this with the possibly substantial legal costs and inconvenience of proceeding with the eviction.

■ Rate arrears

Failure to pay business rates is a criminal, rather than civil, offence and the amount you owe is not subject to negotiation. You must pay your rates as rates are a form of taxation. The local authority will not (indeed cannot) write off rate arrears. However, this does not mean that you cannot reach an agreement with the local authority regarding the form and timing of payment. You can also apply to the ratings office of the local authority for a rates reduction, say because of changed environmental circumstances.

■ Services

Gas and electricity can be cut off if you do not pay your bills, without the need for a court order. Then you are taken to court for the amount outstanding. If you cannot settle your gas and electricity accounts, then either you must choose to do without these services (and eventually pay substantial reconnection charges) or negotiate with the gas or electricity authorities with a view to settling the arrears over a protracted period. Alternatively, if yours is a one-person firm with tiny premises, you could arrange for slot meters to be installed, pre-set so as to recover some of the accumulated arrears from each coin put in the meter.

Similar considerations apply to telephone bills. It is unlikely that you will be disconnected, provided you inform your phone company about your current financial difficulties and negotiate a special arrangement to clear your outstanding balance.

DEALING WITH CREDITORS

You can afford to ignore the first couple of reminders from a creditor, but not thereafter. If you are in real trouble, you should write to each major creditor offering an excuse for not paying, outlining what you intend to do to settle outstanding balances. Explain that, for example:

- you are awaiting some large payments from your own customers and are actively pursuing them for the money they owe you, including threatening them with legal action;
- you have not been able to produce an important order because of non-availability of raw materials;
- a strike among suppliers or distributors has temporarily disrupted your operations;
- the business depends crucially on your own personal inputs and that you have recently been ill.

■ Show commitment

Say that you are fully committed to settling your debts and apologise for the inconvenience you are causing. Offer whatever interim payment you can reasonably afford and specify when you anticipate being in a position to pay the remainder. Obviously you need to pay relatively more to the most potentially troublesome of your creditors, but do offer something to everyone. If a creditor starts charging you interest on unsettled balances, then compare the cost of paying this (though check with an accountant or other professional adviser whether or not the creditor is legally entitled to charge interest under

239

that particular contract) with the interest cost of a bank loan, bearing in mind the need to offer security against a formal bank loan.

These letters are guaranteed to trigger telephone calls from creditors. Prepare for this, and use the conversations as opportunities to reinforce your case for deferring payment. Ask for a discount on the sum outstanding. The creditor is unlikely to agree, but will at least have something to think about instead of contemplating legal action. Creditors want their money and are usually aware of the costs and inconvenience of court proceedings, so you lose little by asking for special consideration.

■ Collection agencies

It is sometimes easier to deal with a debt-collection agency than with the firm to which you originally owed money. If the agency has 'purchased' the debt, it will have done so at a considerable discount (say half the book value of the debt), so it can still make a profit by accepting an offer of partial settlement. Alternatively, the agency might have taken the debt on a commission basis and, thus, will normally be willing to reschedule your repayments over a longer period, providing its total commission is not affected.

■ Payments moratoria

As a last resort, consider discussing with your major suppliers the possibility of a payments moratorium, whereby creditors agree to a delay (three months, for example) in the settlement of outstanding balances. Creditors promise not to take legal action in the interim, but do not forgo their right to sue eventually.

Payments moratoria are best arranged by a professional adviser (such as a solicitor, accountant or bank manager) as creditors will usually insist that an independent outside party supervise the arrangement.

■ *Explain your problems*

Write to creditors in the manner previously outlined. Explain the sources of your problems and the crisis measures you are implementing. Say that your professional adviser (who might actually draft the letter) will collect and hold all the money you receive during the period of the moratorium. Offer to pay off some part of the debt owing to each creditor after a certain period (the end of the second month, for instance) and suggest an intended timescale for settling remaining balances.

■ *The advantages*

This puts the ball firmly in your creditors' court. Asking for a moratorium has several advantages:

- creditors are made aware of your difficulties and the fact that you seriously intend to rescue the business;
- they realise there is little point in their taking legal action against your firm;
- you demonstrate your integrity and you gain time in which to restructure your finances.

In your letter, emphasise your need for increased revenue and include an offer to provide them with goods or services at a special discount and/or to give commission for any business with third parties they secure on your behalf. Of course, a creditor may choose to petition for your bankruptcy, but this will happen anyway if you simply continue to ignore demands for settlement of your debts.

A bankruptcy petition (see Chapter 12) is more likely if you possess many assets that could be liquidated to settle outstanding balances. In this case, you may need to mortgage (see below) some or all of these assets to your creditors as a gesture of goodwill.

■ Hire purchase

Your firm may not sell equipment obtained on hire purchase as it does not belong to you until all instalments have been paid. If you default on payment, the goods can be reclaimed (although a court order is needed once you have paid some minimum amount – see Chapter 9). This might be the best thing from your point of view. Also, the hirer may be anxious to negotiate a system of lower repayments over a longer period in view of the difficulty of rehiring second-hand equipment, plus the costs and inconveniences involved.

■ Loan sharks

If yours is a very small, single-person business, financed entirely by yourself and you have been foolish enough to fall into the hands of a loan shark who charges exorbitant interest for short-term loans, the best thing, usually, is to write to the lender, advising them that you are unable to repay the loan and suggesting that the lender take action through the County court. Then you can ask the court for a repayment schedule suited to your particular circumstances (see Chapter 9).

LOANS FROM BANKS

If you are frank and honest with your bank manager, then they are unlikely to take you to court. Banks greatly prefer to negotiate reasonable arrangements with customers than enforce court actions. Explain your circumstances, and ask for help. Never ignore warning letters from the bank. If you do, the local branch will simply refuse to honour your cheques and refer the case to its regional office, whereupon legal action will be taken to recover the loan. Once your cheques begin to bounce, your credit rating collapses. Two major options are possible:

> *If you are frank and honest with your bank manager, then they are unlikely to take you to court. Banks greatly prefer to negotiate reasonable arrangements with customers than enforce court actions.*

- ■ rescheduling of repayments;
- ■ further loans.

■ Rescheduling of repayments

This might involve converting one type of loan into another – say, from a loan with conventional monthly repayments to a loan that requires only the interest (and nothing from the capital sum advanced) to be paid in the first year of the loan's duration. Equally, the bank may be prepared to change an existing overdraft (repayable on demand) into a fixed-term, fixed-interest loan. You save quite a lot on bank charges here because your current account ceases to be in deficit, although you pay more interest in total.

■ Further loans

You might take out further loans to clear existing repayment arrears and provide finance for future operations. Such loans will have to be secured against your own and/or the business' assets. The question of security therefore deserves further consideration.

SECURITY

The bank will want to know the precise purpose for which the requested sum is intended, and will require comprehensive cash flow forecasts that demonstrate your firm's probable ability to repay the loan on schedule. Also, a detailed business revival plan (as outlined in Chapter 9) should accompany the application. As well as studying your firm's immediate prospects, the bank will also consider your personal skills and qualities, especially your prospects for paid employment if – despite everything – the business does eventually go under. From the bank's perspective, a 'good' security is one that is quickly realisable, keeps its value and adequately covers the loan. Certain securities have market values. Banks will not advance 100 per cent of the current market values of such assets because market prices fluctuate and the bank will fear falls in market price. The commonest means of providing security against loans are outlined below.

■ Life assurance policies

You can assign to the bank the rights to which you are entitled under an existing life assurance policy. Thus, you continue to pay the premiums, but, if you die, the bank and not your next of kin receives the benefits of the policy. If you default on the premiums, the bank liquidates the policy at its surrender value (which the bank will ensure fully covers the loan before advancing any money against it). Note that you lose heavily in terms of the value of your past contributions if the policy is, in fact, surrendered.

Banks are usually willing to take life assurance policies as security because of their straightforward nature, relative to other assets. They are reliable, customers understand what is going on and few legal formalities or administrative costs are necessary. You will be required, however, to furnish the bank with confidential personal information and, perhaps, undertake a medical examination as the bank needs to protect itself against customers failing to disclose to their insurance companies 'material facts', or, lying about their health in order to obtain a policy. (Insurance companies will not honour policies in these circumstances.)

■ Land and buildings

The bank may take a mortgage on your property or, perhaps, a debenture secured against certain of your assets. A mortgage is a 'conveyance' (transfer) of an interest in property as security for debt. Mortgages may be 'legal' or 'equitable'. Under a legal mortgage, the bank assumes legal ownership of the property, which it can sell as it wishes. With an equitable mortgage, the bank has claim to the property, but may not sell it. (Equitable mortgages can be used where someone else already has an interest in the same property.) Normally, the bank will want to have a legal mortgage.

■ Debentures

Debentures usually apply to limited companies. A debenture is a loan to a company conditional on the debenture holder obtaining sufficient of the company's assets to settle the loan if the borrower defaults on repayment. Normally, the bank will require the debenture to be secured against specific named assets (such as equipment or premises owned by the firm), in which case, the security is known as a 'fixed' charge against the firm's assets. If the business is a limited company, then 'floating' charges may also be used, in which case the loan is secured against all the company's assets. In the latter case, however, the bank has no right to claim specific assets if the business fails. Instead, it must take its place alongside the rest of the company's creditors and may receive only partial settlement.

■ Stocks and shares

If you own stocks and shares, you can offer them as security, although the bank will only advance a portion of their current market value because of uncertainties caused by fluctuations in market prices.

■ Guarantees

Here, a third party agrees to be personally responsible for the debts of another person or business. If you trade as a limited company, the bank will normally insist that you personally guarantee the repayment of any loans it makes to the company, and the guarantee will probably have to be secured against your home and/or other personal assets. If you are married, your spouse has a claim on half the house, so the bank may demand that your spouse also sign the guarantee in order to provide the bank with complete indemnity. Before accepting a guarantee, the bank will carefully examine your financial status and debt history.

Another means of providing security is to give the bank the right to reclaim and sell the goods that you purchased with the loan should you fail to repay the money. Banks are typically reluctant to enter this sort of arrangement (sometimes referred to as 'hypothecation' of a loan) because they have neither possession nor control of the goods and so they must rely on your willingness to hand them over – complete and undamaged – following your default

OTHER CRISIS MEASURES

Instead of offering a life assurance policy as security against a loan, you could cash it in at its surrender value. However, think carefully before doing this and note that this option is not available if the policy has already been used as security for an existing debt. Surrender values are usually low (certainly much less than the amount you will already have contributed), and you might desperately need this money for personal use if your business does eventually go under.

■ Do you really need a car?

Try, instead, to economise on operating costs and to raise cash by selling non-essential assets. Do you really need a car, for example?

The sale of a vehicle can raise a couple of thousand pounds, and public transport – while inconvenient – can be used during an immediate short-term crisis. Consider daily or weekly car hire as a temporary alternative to having your own vehicle.

■ Credit cards

Interest rates on credit cards are enormously high, so you should never use credit cards for long-term financing. Nevertheless, judicious timing of purchasing using credit cards can provide short-term relief to a small business experiencing moderate cash flow difficulties. Credit card companies will reschedule the payments of users whose credit card debts get out of control, but will insist that no further use be made of the facility.

SELLING OUT

If you are approached by an outsider interested in purchasing your business, then, clearly, the firm is not without value. Perhaps you can suggest a merger rather than outright sale, especially if the other party is a competitor, in which case you will already know each other's strengths, problems and business methods. Such a merger might enable you to tackle new or bigger projects jointly and markets that were previously inaccessible because of your limited resources and lack of experience and expertise.

Note, also, the possibility of approaching a very large company that might welcome the opportunity of incorporating your firm into its overall supply or distribution system. The buyer will impose its own administrative routines on the business, and you will probably become an employee (subject to PAYE and Class 1 National Insurance contributions) of the takeover company, subject to its day-to-day control. However, at least you will have an income and continue to manage the firm.

■ A going concern

In the case of a straight sale, you want, if possible, to sell your business as a 'going concern' as the market value of an ongoing business is invariably higher than one that is not operational. The firm has existing products (each with its own unique attributes and selling points), machinery and/or office furniture and equipment, customers, a distribution system, suppliers, a business image, product brands and premises. The purchaser of the firm is thus saved considerable start-up expenses, the costs of acquiring capital assets and the need to establish new business and product images.

■ How much is a business worth?

Valuing a business is not easy, yet you need to be able to establish a provisional valuation figure before negotiations can even begin. Also, you might wish to consider winding up your present business and buying another, more profitable, firm that you will have to value to establish whether or not it represents a good purchase. Ultimately, the only way to value a business properly is to put it up for sale and observe the offers that result. It is possible to auction a business, simply accepting the highest bid, but the procedure is not common. Usually, therefore, you must compute an initial benchmark figure and advertise the business at this price or, perhaps, phrase this along the lines of 'offers invited from' and state a minimum value.

There are two fundamental approaches to valuation. One assesses value from the assets the business possesses, the other from the earnings it can create.

VALUING ASSETS

The true values of a business' owned assets are not necessarily reflected in its books. Fixed assets are depreciated annually at the rate that is most tax-efficient, not the rate that most accurately reflects their loss in worth. Thus, valuable fixed assets can remain within a business long after they have theoretically ceased to exist – that is, when they have been completely 'written off' in accounting terms. This is frequently the case with motor vehicles, machines and certain items of furniture.

Equally, certain assets might be massively overpriced, so you should never even consider buying a business merely on the basis of its balance sheet – inspect its physical assets personally, and make sure that all the assets offered for inspection actually belong to the firm.

■ Valuing current assets

Valuation of current assets (stock, debtors, cash) is just as difficult. Everyone in business knows that some debtors will not settle their bills, yet establishing which particular debtors will default and the extent of subsequent losses is extremely difficult. You must examine the structure of outstanding debts, especially the periods for which certain debts have remained unsettled and why long-standing debts have not been cleared. The 'cash' figure in a balance sheet represents cash available on the date the balance sheet was compiled – it might all be spent a week later!

Book values thus represent little more than a starting point for true valuation. Thereafter, you need to assess the business' worth either for its 'break-up' value or as a going concern.

■ *Break-up value*

This means the aggregate of the selling prices of the firm's disposable assets on dissolution of the business, after deducting selling costs such as estate agents' fees when disposing of property, costs of transporting goods to points of sale, expenses of sales people and so on. The past ability of assets to generate earnings within the firm is ignored.

■ *The value of a going concern*

Here you examine not so much the sales potential of individual items, but, rather, the firm's total capacity to create new earnings and growth. Two plus two often equals more than four in these circumstances. Land and buildings, for example, may be worth considerably more when plant and equipment have already been installed and are working than when the land and buildings have to be sold in isolation.

■ Investments

Investments in stocks, shares and debentures might also be worth more when viewed from a going concern perspective. A firm's portfolio of equity investments, for example, will have a low book value immediately after a stock market crash, yet may still offer a sound and potentially lucrative long-term investment for a firm that is able to hold on to its stocks and shares until they recover their value. Similarly, a long overdue debt owing to the firm will raise little if sold to a debt collector, but might be paid in full if the firm continues in operation and can thus wait for its eventual settlement. Stock that is just about to be converted into saleable finished products is worth potentially more than stock that has to be auctioned immediately.

■ Goodwill

The difference between the value of a firm's assets and its sale price is referred to as 'goodwill', which is actually realised only at the moment of the firm's purchase. It represents the worth of the business attributable to it being a going concern, including:

- its good name;
- brand images;
- existing customers and suppliers;
- access to markets and skilled labour;
- the state of its order books and similar attributes independent of physical possessions.

Note that the value of goodwill fluctuates as trading conditions alter. An economic recession, emergence of a new competitor, adverse press or other publicity, or a change in public taste or fashion can quickly wipe out a business' goodwill.

■ *Estimating goodwill*

Estimating goodwill is problematical. Essentially, you have to predict the firm's minimum net profits over, say, the next three years, add to this the expected break-up value of the business in three years' time and then ask how much you would have to invest today in a safe, interest-earning asset (a building society account, for instance) in order to earn these revenues. Suppose, for example, that I expect a business to yield £20,000 a year net profit after tax for each of the next 3 years (thereafter I have no idea of likely trading prospects, so I only consider a three-year period) and that I anticipate being able to sell the firm's physical assets for £30,000 in 3 years' time. The interest rate on building society deposits (after tax) is currently 6 per cent and I have no reason to expect this to alter significantly over the next couple of years. To generate the £90,000 I expect from the business (that is, 3 x £20,000 + £30,000), I would need to put £75,566 into the building society today and leave it there for 3 years (see Note 3). I ignore the possibility of investing the business' first year's £20,000 profit in an interest-bearing deposit account for the next 2 years and of investing the second year's profit intact for a further year. You can take these possibilities into account if you wish, but you then need to do more calculations.

On these assumptions, I would be crazy to pay more than £75,566 for this business, because I can achieve the forecast minimum return by simply depositing the same amount in the building society, at no risk. It seems to me, therefore, that £50,000 is a reasonable figure on which to base negotiations – less if I expect the interest rate to rise (see Note 3).

SUMMARY

Severe financial difficulties require a drastic response. Keep calm, be rational and tackle your problems systematically. Accept that you may have to surrender capital assets, but realise that there are still many things you can do to save the firm. Establish priorities and initiate crisis measures for coping with serious deficits in your cash flow.

Place an embargo on all new capital spending and look for emergency means of raising funds. Consider taking a temporary part-time job, and, if you own your premises, investigate the feasibility of a sale and leaseback arrangement. Perhaps you can increase your personal mortgage or otherwise raise money secured on property owned by yourself or the firm.

Extending the period you take to settle your bills might usefully constitute your first line of defence, although you should beware of the possibility of creditors suspending delivery of vital supplies to the business.

You might be able to get away with not paying your rent or mortgage repayments for a couple of months, but will face eviction in the longer term.

Creditors may be sympathetic to requests for accommodation, provided you make a sincere and sensible approach and demonstrate your intention to eventually clear outstanding debts. Explain to each creditor the reasons for your financial problems, asking for an extended period in which to pay. In really grave circumstances, you might need to employ a solicitor or accountant to request a payments moratorium for unsettled bills.

Your bank could be your biggest friend in this sort of situation. It can offer advice, may be prepared to reschedule the repayment of existing loans, and might even lend you more money, provided appropriate security can be found.

✓ Checklist

- ☐ Have you a contingency plan for dealing with a serious cash flow deficit?

- ☐ How well do you know the creditors to whom you owe most money?

- ☐ Might it be possible to convert your premises into smaller units?

- ☐ How quickly could you sublet part of your premises?

- ☐ Does your lease contain a rent review clause and, if so, do you understand its provisions?

- ☐ If you were to stop paying your rent, how soon do you think you would be evicted from your premises?

- ☐ What is the extent of the security you can offer against a loan?

- ☐ Could you do without your firm's car for a short period?

- ☐ For how much do you think you could sell your business in its present state? What is your estimate of the goodwill of the business?

Notes

1. Property 'licences' offer a more flexible means of letting commercial property than is available using the traditional lease. The conditions embodied within a licence are usually similar to those of a typical lease, but offer minimal security of tenure as licences do not imply any legal interest in premises and, thus, are not covered by the Landlord and Tenant Act 1987. Also, you cannot sell a licence at a premium as you can an orthodox lease.

2. This is nothing more than 'compound interest' in reverse. The compound interest formula is:

$$A = P(1+R)^n$$

where A is the amount at the end of the period, P is the principal invested today, R is the interest rate and 'n' the number of years of the investment. Thus:

$$P = \frac{A}{(1+R)^n} = \frac{90,000}{(1.06)^3} = £75,566$$

3. A common rule of thumb for calculating goodwill is to compute the average difference between the profits of the business and the interest that would have been earned by depositing an amount equal to the value of the business' assets in, say, a building society account for the last three years and multiplying this by three. Then the break-up value of the firm's assets is added to the resulting figure to give the price at which the firm is offered for sale.

Thinking about
the unthinkable

1
2
3
4
5
6
7
8
9
10
11
12

INTRODUCTION

If you are up to your neck in debt and there is absolutely no hope of the business succeeding, you must confront the unpleasant reality of having to close down. Previous chapters have suggested ways of helping you avoid this predicament – lots of stop-gap survival measures were outlined and several hints and strategies offered for repositioning and promoting your product. Nevertheless, despite the very best efforts of their owners, some businesses do go under, so it would be improper of me not to tell you about the circumstances in which bankruptcy and company liquidation occur and the procedures attached to the dissolution of a small firm.

BANKRUPTCY AND COMPANY LIQUIDATION

Sole traders or partners in a business without limited liability can be declared 'bankrupt' by a County court. If, on the other hand, you have formed a limited company then it is the company that is 'liquidated' – as an independent legal entity in its own right – and you are not personally responsible for the company's debts beyond the value of your shareholding in the company. Bankrupts, conversely, must use personal assets and future earnings to pay off business debts. They stand to lose their houses, furniture, vehicles and other 'non-essential' possessions (although the court ultimately determines what constitutes a non-essential possession). Note, importantly, that most banks will not lend to a limited company unless at least one company director personally guarantees the loan's repayment, if necessary from their private estate. Such loans are typically secured against specific personal assets (houses or cars, for example), which are seized if the company fails to redeem the loan.

■ What bankruptcy means

Bankruptcy law in the UK follows the principle that, although a bankrupt person must use their personal wealth to settle outstanding debt, the bankrupt should be free of these liabilities and, thus, able to start another business following the expiry of a 'reasonable' period.

You can be declared bankrupt if you run your own sole trader business or share ownership or responsibility of any firm that does not have limited liability. If, as a partner in a business, you have more money than other partners, then the firm's creditors will probably come gunning for you before they go after the others. Creditors are not concerned that seizing your personal assets and not those of your partners will mean that you make a disproportionately high contribution to settling the partnership's total debts – they just want their money.

■ The bankruptcy petition

A bankruptcy petition differs from an enforcement order (see Chapter 5) in that whereas the latter seeks settlement of a specific proven debt (for example, by seizure of particular physical assets), bankruptcy is the requirement that the debtor settle all outstanding debts – the totality of the debtor's income and assets being taken from the debtor and managed by a trustee appointed by the court specifically for this purpose. Thus, petitions for you to be declared bankrupt are especially likely in the following circumstances:

- several creditors have not been paid and, realising you are unlikely to settle any of their accounts, they get together to recover as much of the money they are owed as possible;
- you have backtracked on settlement of a single (perhaps substantial) proven debt and the creditor uses the threat of the public humiliation associated with bankruptcy proceedings as a means of extracting payment;
- creditors believe you are concealing the true extent of your personal assets;
- an enforcement order has not been honoured and the creditor involved wishes to punish you (and recoup at least some money) by having you publicly disgraced as a bankrupt;
- a small creditor thinks you will use whatever money you have to settle larger debts with what to you are more important suppliers at the expense of the small creditor and, thus, petitions for bankruptcy as a means of obtaining compensation.

An important factor in a creditor's decision to try and have you declared bankrupt is that your formal bankruptcy automatically provides the creditor with sufficient evidence that a debt is 'bad' so that it can be written off in respect of tax and VAT.

■ What you stand to lose

Once you become aware of impending bankruptcy, it is unlawful for you to get rid of valuable assets by giving them away or selling them cheaply to close friends or relatives with the intention of recovering them later. Moreover, the official receiver (who is a court official) is empowered to seize such assets, regardless of the name in which they are held. The court, acting on the official receiver's advice, decides which of your goods (including household goods) you and your family need in order to survive and confiscates the rest.

Courts' estimates of 'need' depend on family circumstances – how many children you have, the presence of an elderly relative or other dependent family member requiring special attention and expenditure and so on. All bank accounts, including joint accounts, are frozen at the point of bankruptcy, and all monies credited to bank and similar accounts are thereafter turned over to the trustee. Note, importantly, that if someone (including your spouse) leaves you money in a will, your family cannot benefit because the amounts received belong to the trustee and not to you. Thus, if you are a bankrupt female parent and your husband dies leaving you all his money, then your children might never see any of that money because it has to be used first to settle your debts. Your husband will probably want to will all his assets directly to the children in these circumstances.

■ *Things that cannot be taken*

You can retain property that you hold in trust for someone else and property held in your spouse's name cannot normally be seized provided:

- you did not transfer the property to your spouse intending to defraud creditors;

- the transfer did not occur within three months of the date of the bankruptcy petition;
- gifts of property to your spouse occurred more than two years before your bankruptcy.

Sales of your assets to other people at low nominal values might not be considered valid in law and the goods involved could be confiscated (unless you can prove you were solvent at the moment the sale was transacted). Goods involved in such deals can be seized if they were sold up to five years prior to a bankruptcy petition (the exact period depends on the nature of the transaction).

■ Avoiding bankruptcy

You might be able to avoid bankruptcy by obtaining an 'administration order' from your local County court. This enables the court to supervise your affairs while you sort out your debts. An administration order is extremely useful if you are being pursued by several creditors, all of whom are using different debt-collection methods. The court protects you from harassment by creditors,

> *You might be able to avoid bankruptcy by obtaining an 'administration order' from your local County court. This enables the court to supervise your affairs while you sort out your debts.*

who are now unable individually to enforce specific claims without the express agreement of the court. In return, you agree to make a fixed monthly payment to the court (which then distributes the money to your creditors equitably) until you clear your debts. You cannot be declared bankrupt while an administration order is in effect unless the court agrees, which is highly unlikely as long as the monthly payments are maintained. To apply for an administration order, you contact the office of your local official receiver, whose address and telephone number are available from your County court.

■ *Deeds of arrangement*

Similarly, you can arrange *an ad hoc* meeting of your creditors at which you try to persuade them to settle for less than they are owed.

This saves them the costs and inconvenience of petitioning for your bankruptcy. However, creditors may conclude that:

- they have nothing to lose in having you declared bankrupt as this ensures that the court administers your affairs;
- bankruptcy is better because they can then write off your debts in the current tax year.

A more realistic approach is therefore to seek a 'deed of arrangement' with creditors, whereby all your business property is legally assigned (registered) to a trustee acceptable to them. The official receiver can arrange for the appointment of a suitable trustee, who then administers your assets on your creditors' behalf. This is a secure, legally founded arrangement that avoids your being declared officially bankrupt.

The deed must be approved by a majority of creditors and is binding on signatories to the deal, but it does not bind creditors who refuse to participate in the arrangement.

Hence, the latter can still petition to have you made bankrupt. All the administrative costs of the process are borne by you.

■ Individual voluntary arrangements (IVAs)

With an IVA, you offer to make partial settlement of accounts owed to creditors (say, 50 pence for every £1 owed). Simultaneously, your assets are made over to a registered insolvency practitioner of your choice. (Insolvency practitioners are normally chartered accountants or solicitors who specialise in insolvency work and are registered with the DTI.) The insolvency practitioner approaches the County court on your behalf and the court issues an 'interim order', which prevents anyone petitioning for your bankruptcy or initiating proceedings against your property for a period of 14 days (or longer at the court's discretion).

A creditors' meeting is held that considers your offer. The creditors may accept the offer by voting in favour with a majority of 75 per cent (by value of the debts owed) of those present or voting by proxy. Additionally, the offer must be accepted by at least half (by value) of all creditors to whom notice of the meeting was sent. If accepted, the IVA is approved by the court and becomes legally binding on all creditors, including any who voted against your offer or did not attend the meeting (provided they were informed that it was taking place).

A problem with this is that, after the meeting, creditors may emerge who were not invited to attend, and these creditors can still take legal action against you, including bankruptcy proceedings.

HOW BANKRUPTCY OCCURS

It is possible to declare yourself bankrupt (through the County court) in order to avoid being served with an enforcement order from a particular creditor. Equally, you can be forced into bankruptcy via a petition from a creditor acting alone or with other creditors. Petitions are not allowed unless you owe at least £750 and have done so for at least 3 months.

Creditors become aware of your uncertain financial position when, despite threats and reminders, their bills remain unpaid for long periods. However, they cannot initiate bankruptcy proceedings unless there is clear evidence of your inability to settle your debts.

Creditors become aware of your uncertain financial position when, despite threats and reminders, their bills remain unpaid for long periods. However, they cannot initiate bankruptcy proceedings unless there is clear evidence of your inability to settle your debts (see Note 1).

Traditionally, courts have accepted the following behaviour as being indicative of personal insolvency:

- if a creditor has obtained a court order requiring a debtor to settle a debt and this order has been served and ignored;
- the debtor informs creditors of their inability to settle debts in full;
- if a debtor deliberately makes themselves inaccessible – say, by changing address, demonstrably intending to avoid creditors;
- the debtor fraudulently transfers property to other people to avoid its possible seizure.

■ Interim receivers

The creditors' first step is to approach the County court and ask for the issue of a 'bankruptcy petition' against you. If the court accepts the request the petition is served on your last known address and a date for hearing the case is determined.

Following the hearing, the petition is either dismissed or accepted. In the latter case, the court appoints an 'interim receiver' to take charge of your affairs. The interim receiver is selected by the court and, typically, will be an accountant, solicitor or insolvency practitioner. This action has the effect of freezing your finances and enables the interim receiver to take immediate possession of your property, pending the appointment of a trustee to manage your assets on behalf of the creditors. Note that a creditor's right to seize any of your assets (the right being obtained under, for example, a warrant of execution, garnishee or similar order – see Chapter 5) is lost at this point, even if you present your own bankruptcy petition. The creditor holding the warrant becomes just another unsecured creditor who will receive proportionately no more or less than others.

■ Formal bankruptcy

Note, importantly, that so far you have still not been adjudged formally bankrupt. This happens only if your creditors refuse any offer you make or if you abscond or if you appear to be hiding your assets or are otherwise deliberately uncooperative. In any of these circumstances, your creditors and the official receiver will jointly ask the court to declare you formally bankrupt. When this happens, the court issues an order depriving you of your property and placing it with a trustee appointed by the creditors and approved by the court, although initially the official receiver undertakes this role, subject to the court's approval

■ *Trustees*

The trustee (usually an accountant) must be someone considered by the court to be a fit and proper person to undertake these duties. Their task is to realise your assets as quickly as possible and distribute the proceeds among creditors. In return, the trustee is rewarded by being paid an agreed percentage of the amount raised. If there are no assets to be realised, the official receiver acts as the trustee.

The examination

You will be required to prepare a full statement of your affairs, listing all your personal assets and liabilities and, if this is demanded by the official receiver, attend a 'public examination' held in open court.

Here you are required to explain the circumstances and causes of your financial difficulties, and answer questions from creditors and/or the official receiver concerning your conduct and the whereabouts of your assets. You have to satisfy the authorities that the cause of your impending bankruptcy did not involve fraud or improper behaviour. The official receiver does not normally require a public examination.

Payment of creditors

Creditors are paid according to the predetermined order specified in the Insolvency Act 1986. 'Secured' creditors (those with direct claims on specific assets, such as a bank loan secured against the firm's premises) are paid first. If the sale of the particular asset specified in a security arrangement (only fixed charges are allowed to sole traders and partnerships – see Chapter 10) fails to raise enough money to pay off a secured debt, then the outstanding balance is pooled with the debts of unsecured creditors and a 'so much in the pound' settlement is applied to this amount. Next come unpaid taxes and local authority rates, followed by employees' pay, then outstanding National Insurance contributions and only then the firm's unsecured creditors.

Partnerships

In partnerships, each partner is treated individually (because the firm is not a separate legal entity), although the fact that one partner is adjudged bankrupt does not necessarily mean that the entire firm must become bankrupt. Here, the bankrupt partner's share of the partnership's property is handed over to the trustee.

If the whole firm goes bankrupt, then, of course, all the partners (excluding registered sleeping partners with limited liability) necessarily become bankrupt.

Undischarged bankrupts are prohibited by law from obtaining credit (beyond very small amounts) without disclosing their bankruptcy. Also, they are not allowed to trade under any other business name unless they simultaneously and openly reveal they are bankrupt under their previous business names. Bankrupts cannot become company directors or be in any way involved in company management.

DISCHARGE

If realisation of your assets raises enough money to settle your debts, you are discharged at that moment. Otherwise, you have to apply to the court for a discharge some time in the future, having demonstrated serious attempts at settling outstanding balances.

There are three ways to obtain a discharge. These are by:

- 'automatic' expiry of a minimum time period;
- 'review';
- early 'application'.

■ Automatic discharge

Discharge occurs automatically for the first-time bankrupt after three years. People who have been bankrupt before may have to wait up to 15 years for automatic discharge.

■ Discharge by review

The County court registrar may suggest at the moment a bankruptcy order is issued that a date be set when the matter might be reconsidered. In the meantime, you have to make regular contributions towards settlement of your debts. If you take a job following your business' collapse, your pay could be subject to an attachment of earnings order (see Chapter 5).

■ Early application

You can apply to the court for early discharge at any time. On receipt of the application (plus the appropriate fee), the court informs:

- the creditors (who may oppose the discharge);
- the trustee;
- the official receiver.

The court may grant immediate discharge or make the discharge conditional on particular events (repaying a certain amount of money, for example) and/or specify that the discharge occur only after a certain period has expired. You must demonstrate to the court that your bankruptcy is causing you exceptional hardship for example, preventing you earning a living).

Discharge means you are free to obtain credit and run a new business. Prior to discharge, however, your legal rights are severely affected. In particular, control over your income and property is exercised by the trustee and you cannot interfere with the trustee's decision. The trustee can sell whichever of your assets they choose and can sue third parties for money that you are owed and keep the proceeds. Undischarged bankrupts cannot be local councillors, stand for Parliament or hold any office that involves handling public money. Many professional bodies (solicitors and accountants, for instance) do not allow bankrupt members to practice.

■ The rights of a spouse

Nowadays, a solvent spouse or dependent relative has the legal right to occupy the family home. Thus, if you are declared bankrupt, but your husband or wife is not, they cannot be evicted in order to sell off the family residential property. However, your 'half' of the family home ceases to belong to you and may be disposed of appropriately. How this will operate in practice has yet to be established. Further complications arise if you are separated or newly divorced or if unequal contributions to the purchase of the home can be proven. Specialist legal advice is necessary in these circumstances.

■ Services and bank accounts

The gas, electricity and telephone companies can cut you off as soon as you are declared bankrupt, unless you have transferred these services into someone else's name.

Your bank account is frozen, though you may open another account without declaring your bankruptcy to your new bank, provided the account is not overdrawn (which is equivalent to your 'obtaining credit' and so is illegal). Note that the official receiver is entitled to confiscate any money you deposit in a new account. Life assurance policies with surrender values will be seized, but pension fund entitlements cannot be taken.

A bankrupt who conceals the existence of personal assets or who falsifies records commits a criminal offence for which they may be imprisoned. Failure to account for assets and/or keep proper records are not criminal offences, but may result in the court refusing to grant a discharge.

COMPANY LIQUIDATION

A company is a separate legal entity and, thus, must be liquidated in its own right, quite independently of its owners (shareholders). All unpaid share capital is called up on liquidation. Thereafter, the principle of limited liability protects shareholders from personal liability for the company's debts.

As with a sole trader, liquidation proceedings can be initiated by the company itself. In this case an extraordinary resolution (requiring the support of 75 per cent of shareholders' votes, or 51 per cent if the company is insolvent) made at an official meeting of the company's shareholders is necessary, and the courts need not be involved.

On liquidation, the company may be solvent or insolvent. If it is solvent (for example, if it was formed for a particular project that has been successfully completed), its members pay off the creditors and simply wind the company up. If it is insolvent, then either:

■ its creditors form a committee to supervise the voluntary winding up;

- one or more creditors present a petition to the court for compulsory liquidation, though, in this case, the amount owed must exceed £750. Note also that a shareholder may ask the court for a compulsory winding up order.

■ Compulsory winding up

Other circumstances in which a company may be compulsorily wound up are:

- if it fails to register its final accounts with the Registrar of Companies;
- if it does not trade for more than a year;
- when the number of its members falls below the statutory minimum of two;
- if a court decides that it is 'just and equitable' that the company be wound up.

Following a compulsory winding up order, the court may appoint its own liquidator or supervise a liquidator appointed by the company or its creditors.

Company liquidation and bankruptcy are essentially similar, although it is obvious from the above that personal bankruptcy is infinitely more painful to the owner(s) of the firm. In the case of a company, it is the company and not you personally that is responsible for the business' debts – your direct liability is restricted to your personal shareholding (normally £100 for a small private company). Clearly, it is wise to become a company if your business is such that its failure might leave you with a large accumulation of debt (although limited companies themselves have serious problems – see Chapter 10). If you do not operate as a limited liability organisation, you should regularly examine trends in your cash flow to assess their implications for your personal financial liability if the business suddenly fails.

The liquidator of a company is equivalent to the trustee of a bankrupt. Instead of the appointment of an interim receiver in bankruptcy, a company has a 'winding up order' issued against it, the effect of which is to place the company's assets in the liquidator's hands. Then, the company has to prepare a statement of affairs, and a meeting of creditors is arranged. Legal actions against the company (such as warrants of execution) are cancelled as soon as the liquidation begins in order to protect all creditors equally.

ADMINISTRATION ORDERS

Administration orders analogous to those used to avoid personal bankruptcy have been possible for companies since 1987, as are compositions (that is, 'so much in the pound' settlements) involving the minimum legal interference and fuss.

The issue of an administration order by the court enables the company to continue trading, albeit under the supervision of an administrator appointed by the court, and the company is not wound up. The administrator acts as the company's agent. They are empowered to:

- borrow money on the company's behalf;
- appoint and dismiss directors;
- sue in the company's name;
- meet with creditors and shareholders and determine changes in the company's organisational structure.

During the period an administration order is in effect, this fact must be stated on all company documents, together with the administrator's name and reason for their appointment.

■ Receivership

If the creditor initiating court action is a debenture holder, whose debenture is secured under a fixed or floating charge (see Chapter 10 and Note 2 below), the court may appoint a 'receiver' rather than an administrator and the company is then said to be 'in receivership'.

The role of a receiver is essentially similar to that of an administrator. Note that it is unusual these days for a company's bankers not to have a fixed or floating charge debenture in respect of substantial loans made to the company, so that banks typically enjoy the right to appoint receivers for insolvent companies.

There can be no public examination of the 'company' as such, although its individual directors may be so examined. Whereas a bankrupt is 'discharged', a company is given an 'order for dissolution'.

■ Charges

Company debts secured against floating charges receive priority over unsecured creditors, but are paid only after:

- fixed charges;
- the costs of liquidation;
- other preferential claims (taxes, wages and National Insurance);

have been settled. Note that, for both company liquidation and personal bankruptcy, a secured creditor who petitions for the business' liquidation or for individual bankruptcy automatically relinquishes their right to possession of the particular secured asset, which is now sold off, with the proceeds going into a general pool for distribution to creditors in the order previously outlined. Other creditors may have equal-ranking secured claims on the firm and will thus share in the money available for secured creditors.

> *Bankruptcy and company liquidation can be emotionally and psychologically harrowing. Remember, though, that some of the most successful business people around are individuals who at some time or another, have had to wind up an enterprise.*

THE WAY AHEAD

Bankruptcy and company liquidation can be emotionally and psychologically harrowing. Remember, though, that some of the most successful business people around are individuals who at some time or another, have had to wind up an enterprise. If your firm has failed, learn from the experience and use it to your best advantage – having failed once you are not likely to make the same mistakes in the future.

SUMMARY

Bankruptcy is bad news – really bad news – and you must avoid it at all costs. Cease trading immediately you suspect that bankruptcy might be a possibility – liquidate your assets and clear your debts. It is simply not worth running the risk of bankruptcy just to try and earn a few extra pounds.

Small businesses with substantial cash flows should become limited companies before they begin to accumulate large amounts of debt. Disadvantages – such as the costs and inconveniences of company formation, the need to employ an accountant to audit the company's books and the requirement that final accounts be available for public inspection – are easily outweighed by the benefits of incorporation in these circumstances.

> Cease trading immediately you suspect that bankruptcy might be a possibility – liquidate your assets and clear your debts. It is simply not worth running the risk of bankruptcy just to try and earn a few extra pounds.

As a bankrupt, you are not allowed to start another new firm without declaring to customers and suppliers that you are a bankrupt and you are personally liable for the failed business' debts. Your spouse and other members of the family will suffer and you could be subjected to the humiliating experience of a public examination in open court.

Yet, if it happens, it happens. Do not be too despondent – learn from your past mistakes and never be afraid to try again.

Notes

1. Such evidence used to be called an 'act of bankruptcy', but this term was abolished in 1986.
2. Non-incorporated businesses must secure loans against specific, named items in the firm's asset structure. Limited companies, in contrast, may secure loans against a floating charge covering any or all of the company's assets, including stock and work in progress, and outstanding debts owed to the business. A floating charge is said to 'hover' over the property until liquidation, at which time it attaches to any assets currently available.

Index